DR. RAY M. FRANK

A NavPress Bible study on the books of

RUTH & ESTHER

NAVPRESS

A MINISTRY OF THE NAVIGATORS
P.O. BOX 35001, COLORADO SPRINGS, COLORADO 80935

The Navigators is an international Christian organization. Jesus Christ gave His followers the Great Commission to go and make disciples (Matthew 28:19). The aim of The Navigators is to help fulfill that commission by multiplying laborers for Christ in every nation.

NavPress is the publishing ministry of The Navigators. NavPress publications are tools to help Christians grow. Although publications alone cannot make disciples or change lives, they can help believers learn biblical discipleship, and apply what they learn to their lives and ministries.

Eighth printing, 1994

Printed in the United States of America

CONTENTS

ACKNOWLEDGMENTS

This LIFECHANGE study has been produced through the coordinated efforts of a team of Navigator Bible study developers and NavPress editorial staff, along with a nationwide network of fieldtesters.

SERIES EDITOR: KAREN HINCKLEY

HOW TO USE THIS STUDY

Objectives

Most guides in the LIFECHANGE series of Bible studies cover one book of the Bible. This one covers two books with similar themes. Although the LIFECHANGE guides vary with the books they explore, they share some common goals:

1. To provide you with a firm foundation of understanding and a thirst to return to the book;

2. To teach you by example how to study a book of the Bible without structured guides;

3. To give you all the historical background, word definitions, and explanatory notes you need, so that your only other reference is the Bible;

4. To help you grasp the message of the book as a whole;

5. To teach you how to let God's Word transform you into Christ's image.

Each lesson in this study is designed to take 60 to 90 minutes to complete on your own. The guide is based on the assumption that you are completing one lesson per week, but if time is limited you can do half a lesson per week or whatever amount allows you to be thorough.

Flexibility

LIFECHANGE guides are flexible, allowing you to adjust the quantity and depth of your study to meet your individual needs. The guide offers many optional questions in addition to the regular numbered questions. The optional questions, which appear in the margins of the study pages, include the following:

Optional Application. Nearly all application questions are optional; we hope you will do as many as you can without overcommitting yourself.

For Thought and Discussion. Beginning Bible students should be able to handle these, but even advanced students need to think about them. These questions frequently deal with ethical issues and other biblical principles. They often offer cross-references to spark thought, but the references do not give obvious answers. They are good for group discussions.

For Further Study. These include: a) cross-references that shed light on a topic the book discusses, and b) questions that delve deeper into the passage. You can omit them to shorten a lesson without missing a major point of the passage.

If you are meeting in a group, decide together which optional questions to prepare for each lesson, and how much of the lesson you will cover at the next meeting. Normally, the group leader should make this decision, but you might let each member choose his or her own application questions.

As you grow in your walk with God, you will find the LIFECHANGE guide growing with you—a helpful reference on a topic, a continuing challenge for application, a source of questions for many levels of growth.

Overview and Details

Lessons one through five and six through ten are each a self-contained study of a book. You can do one right after the other or do something else in between. Each study begins with an overview of the book. The key to interpretation is context—what is the whole passage or book *about*?—and the key to context is purpose—what is the author's *aim* for the whole work? In lessons one and six you will lay the foundation for your study of each book by asking yourself, "Why did the author (and God) write the book? What did they want to accomplish? What is the book about?"

In lessons two through four and seven through nine you will analyze successive passages in detail. Thinking about how a paragraph fits into the overall goal of the book will help you to see its purpose. Its purpose will help you see its meaning. Frequently reviewing a chart or outline of the book will enable you to make these connections.

Finally, in lessons five and ten, you will review each book, returning to the big picture to see whether your view of it has changed after closer study. Review will also strengthen your grasp of major issues and give you an idea of how you have grown from your study.

Kinds of Questions

Bible study on your own—without a structured guide—follows a progression. First you observe: What does the passage *say*? Then you interpret: What does the passage *mean*? Lastly you apply: How does this truth affect my life?

Some of the "how" and "why" questions will take some creative thinking, even prayer, to answer. Some are opinion questions without clearcut right answers; these will lend themselves to discussions and side studies.

Don't let your study become an exercise of knowledge alone. Treat the passage as God's Word, and stay in dialogue with Him as you study. Pray, "Lord, what do you want me to see here?" "Father, why is this true?" "Lord, how does this apply to my life?"

It is important that you write down your answers. The act of writing clarifies your thinking and helps you to remember.

Meditating on verses is an option in several lessons. Its purpose is to let biblical truth sink into your inner convictions so that you will increasingly be able to act on this truth as a natural way of life. You may want to find a quiet place to spend five minutes each day repeating the verse(s) to yourself. Think about what each word, phrase, and sentence means to you. At intervals throughout the rest of the day, remind yourself of the verse(s).

Study Aids

A list of reference materials, including a few notes of explanation to help you make good use of them, begins on page 117. This guide is designed to include enough background to let you interpret with just your Bible and the guide. Still, if you want more information on a subject or want to study a book on your own, try the references listed.

Scripture Versions

Unless otherwise indicated, the Bible quotations in this guide are from the New International Version of the Bible. Other versions cited are the Revised Standard Version (RSV), the New American Standard Bible (NASB), and the King James Version (KJV).

Use any translation you like for study, preferably more than one. A paraphrase such as The Living Bible is not accurate enough for study, but it can be helpful for comparison or devotional reading.

Memorizing and Meditating

A psalmist wrote, "I have hidden your word in my heart that I might not sin against you" (Psalm 119:11). If you write down a verse or passage that challenges or encourages you, and reflect on it often for a week or more, you will find it beginning to affect your motives and actions. We forget quickly what we read once; we remember what we ponder.

When you find a significant verse or passage, you might copy it onto a card to keep with you. Set aside five minutes during each day just to think about what the passage might mean in your life. Recite it over to yourself, exploring its meaning. Then, return to your passage as often as you can during your day, for a brief review. You will soon find it coming to mind spontaneously.

For Group Study

A group of four to ten people allows the richest discussions, but you can adapt this guide for other sized groups. It will suit a wide range of group types, such as home Bible studies, growth groups, youth groups, and businessmen's studies. Both new and experienced Bible students, and new and mature Christians, will benefit from the guide. You can omit or leave for later years any questions you find too easy or too hard.

The guide is intended to lead a group through one lesson per week. However, feel free to split lessons if you want to discuss them more thoroughly. Or, omit some questions in a lesson if preparation or discussion time is limited. You can always return to this guide for personal study later. You will be able to discuss only a few questions at length, so choose some for discussion and others for background. Make time at each discussion for members to ask about anything they didn't understand.

Each lesson in the guide ends with a section called "For the group." These sections give advice on how to focus a discussion, how you might apply the lesson in your group, how you might shorten a lesson, and so on. The group leader should read each "For the group" at least a week ahead so that he or she can tell the group how to prepare for the next lesson.

Each member should prepare for a meeting by writing answers for all of the background and discussion questions to be covered. If the group decides not to take an hour per week for private preparation, then expect to take at least two meetings per lesson to work through the questions. Application will be very difficult, however, without private thought and prayer.

Two reasons for studying in a group are accountability and support. When each member commits in front of the rest to seek growth in an area of life, you can pray with one another, listen jointly for God's guidance, help one another to resist temptation, assure each other that the other's growth matters to you, use the group to practice spiritual principles, and so on. Pray about one another's commitments and needs at most meetings. Spend the first few minutes of each meeting sharing any results from applications prompted by previous lessons. Then discuss new applications toward the end of the meeting. Follow such sharing with prayer for these and other needs.

If you write down each other's applications and prayer requests, you are more likely to remember to pray for them during the week, ask about them at the next meeting, and notice answered prayers. You might want to get a notebook for prayer requests and discussion notes.

Notes taken during discussion will help you to remember, follow up on ideas, stay on the subject, and clarify a total view of an issue. But don't let note-taking keep you from participating. Some groups choose one member at each meeting to take notes. Then someone copies the notes and distributes them at the next meeting. Rotating these tasks can help include people. Some groups have someone take notes on a large pad of paper or erasable marker board (pre-formed shower wallboard works well), so that everyone can see what has been recorded.

Pages 119-121 list some good sources of counsel for leading group studies. The *Small Group Letter,* published by NavPress, is unique, offering insights from experienced leaders every other month.

OVERVIEW

The Story of Ruth

Map of Israel Under the Judges

"In those days Israel had no king; everyone did as he saw fit."

Judges 17:6, 21:25

The story of Ruth shines like a diamond in the dark years before Israel took Saul as its king. On one level, it is a tale of selfless love in a family, but at bottom it tells what God was doing when most of His people were doing whatever they pleased.

9

TIMELINE FOR THE BOOK OF RUTH

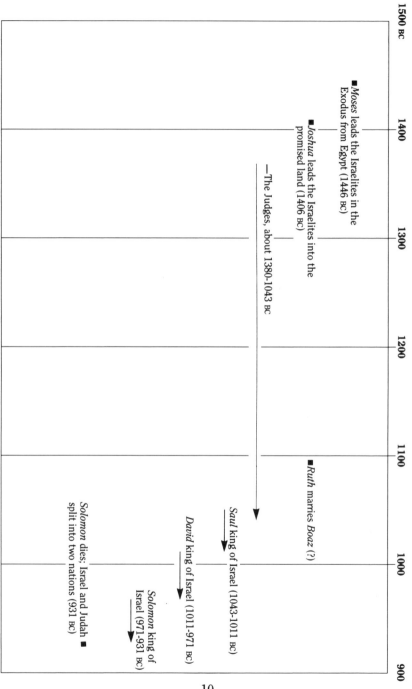

1500 BC — 1400 — 1300 — 1200 — 1100 — 1000 — 900

■ *Moses* leads the Israelites in the Exodus from Egypt (1446 BC)

■ *Joshua* leads the Israelites into the promised land (1406 BC)

—The Judges, about 1380-1043 BC

■ *Ruth* marries *Boaz* (?)

Saul king of Israel (1043-1011 BC)

David king of Israel (1011-971 BC)

Solomon king of Israel (971-931 BC)

Solomon dies; Israel and Judah ■ split into two nations (931 BC)

10

The judges

After Moses died, Joshua led the Israelites into the promised land. They were supposed to kill or enslave all the Canaanites, lest those people seduce Israel into their depraved, pagan ways (Deuteronomy 7:1-6). But the conquest was incomplete when Joshua died, and the Israelites found it more agreeable to settle down among the Canaanites, trade and intermarry with them, and borrow their morals and religious beliefs.

God had promised Israel victory over the Canaanites if His people remained faithful to Him, but defeat and enslavement if they shared their loyalties with other gods. The book of Judges shows a repeating cycle of apostasy, oppression by foreign peoples, appeals for help, and deliverance by the ever-faithful Lord. What the Israelites saw at the time, however, was an endless series of skirmishes and raids interspersed with months or years of tense peace. The "judges" who arose were men (and one woman) endowed by God with special skills to lead the tribes. They were chiefly empowered to lead in warfare, but God also gifted them with wisdom, discernment, and moral virtue.

When a judge defeated an enemy, there was often peace in his region for a generation. He was respected as one who could decide disputes between people, and he might influence some Israelites to conform their religion and ethics more to God's Law. However, no judge ever governed more than a few of the twelve tribes of Israel. Israel was just a loose league of tribes; the mountains and Canaanite cities that separated them prevented unified action. Hence, while there was peace and godliness briefly in one tribe, parts of another tribe were practicing child sacrifice and ritual prostitution with their pagan neighbors, and another several tribes were at war with foreigners.

Judah, where the book of Ruth is set, seldom appears in the book of Judges. No judge over Judah is named, and no battle for liberation is described. Judges 15:9-13 tells us that in the time of Samson the Philistines dominated Judah and the tribe accepted its foreign rulers. The Judahites "mustered a force, not to support Samson, but to capture him for the Philistines."[1] The Philistines worshiped the gods Dagon ("Grain," a god of the crops) and Baal-

Zebul ("Baal the Prince," a god of rain and thunder). However, Bethlehem in the book of Ruth shows no signs of war or Philistine influence; the village is like an island in a sea of violence and immorality.

We can date Ruth's life only approximately. Her great-grandson David became king of Judah in 1011 BC at the age of thirty,[2] so Ruth and Boaz probably married around 1100-1075 BC.

The monarchy

Because Ruth 4:22 names David, we know that the book was written sometime after he became king of Israel. In his lifetime and that of his son Solomon, Israel finally defeated the Canaanites and attained the peace and prosperity Moses had promised. After Solomon, most of Israel rejected the royal house of David, but Judah continued to adore him and crown his descendants. When peace and prosperity crumbled, Judah looked back to David's time as a golden age. The book of Ruth was written by someone who revered David, but it could have been anyone who lived after 1000 BC. Because of the book's literary style, most scholars suggest dates between 1000 and 600 BC, while Judah was still ruled by kings from David's line.[3] However, the story itself is probably a tradition passed down in Ruth's and David's family, since the tale so vividly reflects the customs of its setting.

Ruth the Moabitess

The author continually reminds us that Ruth was a not an Israelite (2:2,6,10,21; 4:5,10). Israel regarded Moab as an inferior people, descended from an incestuous union (Genesis 19:30-38). The Law stated that "No Ammonite or Moabite or any of his descendants may enter the assembly of the LORD, even down to the tenth generation" (Deuteronomy 23:3) because Ammon and Moab had been hostile toward Israel since the days of Moses. Moab oppressed some of the Israelite tribes for eighteen years toward the beginning of the judges' era (Judges 3:12-30). When threatened by King Saul, David sent his parents (Ruth's grandson and his

12

wife) to the king of Moab for protection (1 Samuel 22:3-4), but when David became king of Israel, he fought and subdued Moab (2 Samuel 8:2). For the next several centuries, Moab alternately won and lost its independence from Israel; the two nations were never at peace until Assyria conquered them both (2 Kings 1:1, 3:4-27, 13:20, 14:25; Isaiah 15:1-9).

This historical enmity and the express command of Scripture make it astonishing that God chose a Moabitess to be the ancestor of both David and Jesus, that the author of the book of Ruth stressed this fact, and that the Jews revered David's ancestress enough to acknowledge the story as Scripture. In light of Deuteronomy 23:3, why was David allowed to be not only a member of the congregation of Israel but even king? Certainly the Israelites of Ruth's day were casual toward God's Law, but why did God select this family above all others? As you study the book of Ruth, keep these questions in mind.

1. The book of Ruth is a story, crafted with artless genius. It demands to be studied not by dissecting it into bits but by appreciating it as a whole. So, begin by reading it through (it has only four chapters), jotting down any important repeated words and phrases you notice, key ideas and themes, and any questions you have about customs, words, and so on. Don't let notetaking distract you from enjoying the story; take notes after your first reading if necessary.

   important repeated words and phrases _____

   _____

   _____

   _____

   _____

   _____

   key ideas and themes _____

   _____

For Thought and Discussion: Both 1:1-5 and 4:13-17, which frame the story, contain 71 words in Hebrew. Compare and contrast these two compact sections. How do they relate to each other and to the rest of the story?

questions _____

_____

2. Now skim the story again and write a title for each episode that tells what it is about.

1:1-5 _____

_____

1:6-22 _____

_____

2:1-23 _____

_____

3:1-18 _____

_____

4:1-12 _____

_____

4:13-17 _____

_____

4:18-22 _____

_____

14

3. Briefly describe your first impressions of the characters.

Naomi _____

_____

_____

Ruth _____

_____

_____

Orpah _____

_____

_____

Boaz _____

_____

_____

the unnamed kinsman in chapter 4 _____

_____

_____

_____

Study Skill—Themes and Purposes
Consciously or unconsciously, we usually study a book of the Bible in light of what we think the book as a whole is about. It is therefore wise to come to some tentative, conscious conclusions about this. In a narrative (true story) like Ruth, we should think about the *plot* (what happens in the story), the *main characters* (who are most important), *themes* (ideas or topics that recur through the book), and the *author's purpose* (what is he trying to explain, convince us about, encourage us to do, or accomplish). A book may have several themes and purposes, and the more of them
(continued on page 16)

(continued from page 15)
we can discern, the more we will benefit from the study.

Bible teachers often recommend that we read a book first for an overview and an initial impression of the themes and purposes. Then, after studying the book in detail, we reconsider our view of the themes and purposes.

4. At this point, what do you think are the main themes of Ruth or the main purposes for which it was written?

_____

_____

_____

_____

_____

_____

_____

_____

_____

5. "In the final analysis, God is the hero of all biblical narratives."[4] What does your first reading of Ruth tell you about God?

_____

_____

_____

_____

_____

_____

_____

_____

6. What lessons can you already see that the book of Ruth has for us? (Think about how the themes and what you learn about God are relevant to you.)

_____

_____

_____

_____

_____

_____

17

For the group

This "For the group" section and the ones in later lessons are intended to suggest ways of structuring your discussions. Feel free to select what suits your group. The main goals of this lesson are to get to know the book of Ruth and the people with whom you are going to study it.

Worship. Some groups like to begin with prayer and/or singing. Some pray only briefly for God's guidance at the beginning, but leave extended prayer until after the study. Ask God to speak to each of you through your discussion of Ruth.

Warm-up. The beginning of a new study is a good time to lay a foundation for honest sharing of ideas, for getting comfortable with each other, and for encouraging a sense of common purpose. One way to establish common ground is to talk about what each group member hopes to get out of your group—out of your study of Ruth, and out of any prayer, singing, sharing, outreach, or anything else you might do together. Discuss also what you hope to give to the group. If you have someone write down each member's hopes and expectations, then you can look back at these goals later to see if they are being met. You can then change your meetings accordingly.

You may decide to take about fifteen minutes at the beginning of your discussion of lesson one to discuss goals. Or, you may prefer to take a whole meeting to hand out study guides, introduce the study, examine the "How to Use This Study" section on pages 5-8, and discuss goals. You can structure a discussion of "How to Use This Study" by reminding the group of the main points from this section and then asking if anyone has questions about what to do.

For example, point out the optional questions in the margins. These are available as group discussion questions, ideas for application, and further study. It is unlikely that anyone will have either the time or desire to answer all the optional questions and do all the applications. It is reasonable to expect a person to do *one* "Optional Application" for any given lesson. You might choose *two* "For Thought and Discussions" for your group discussion. If someone wants to write answers to the optional questions, suggest that he use a separate notebook. It will also be helpful for discussion notes, prayer requests, answers to prayers, application plans, and so on.

Note the observation-interpretation-application pattern in each lesson. Many of the numbered questions are observations and basic interpretations that lay the groundwork for deeper study. The meaty questions are often in the margins. In your group discussion, you may prefer to move quickly through the numbered questions (even skipping some) in order to concentrate on questions that interest you.

Point out the study aids on pages 117-121. If you own any, bring them in to show the group.

You may need to discuss how and why Christians memorize and meditate on Scripture. Christian meditation is not meant to empty the mind, as in oriental mysticism. Rather, after emptying your mind of distractions, you fill it with God's thoughts by dwelling on a short piece of His Word.

First impressions. Start with a question that everyone can answer, like "What did you like best about the book of Ruth?" Then use questions 1-5 to get a broad sense of what the book is about. It is often dull to ask, "What did you get for number 1? . . . 2? . . ." It is more interesting for the group if you rephrase the questions: "What repeated words did you find? What is Boaz like? Can someone describe Naomi?"

Your goal is for everyone to get a general grasp of the book's themes and for everyone to sense the characters as real people. It will be easier for you to make applications if you try to identify with each character.

Application. You'll find more Study Skills on application in later lessons (pages 28, 33, 41, 82, and 97). If the group finds application difficult, you can look ahead at those Study Skills. Otherwise, take at least ten minutes to discuss how one theme of Ruth applies to you. Try to find at least one way in which your situation is like Ruth's, Naomi's, or Boaz's.

If group members do not know each other well, they may be reluctant to discuss specific circumstances in their lives. Instead of forcing intimacy too soon, spend the next few weeks building trust

19

among yourselves. You may want to lay some ground rules, such as that no information learned from a prayer request or application may be repeated outside the group.

Questions. Give the group a chance to voice any questions about the book of Ruth or the time of the judges. You may decide to postpone answering some questions until after you have studied the book in more detail, but you may want to assign certain people to research answers to some questions. The sources on pages 117-121 may help. It's often easiest to let the group leader do all the research, but the group will mature together if other members are encouraged and helped to share this responsibility.

Wrap-up. This is a time to bring the discussion to a focused end and to make any announcements about the next lesson or meeting.

Worship. A time of prayer rounds out a meeting. You can share requests as a group or break up into smaller groups of two, three, or four. If group members don't feel comfortable praying aloud, you can pray silently for a while, and then the leader can close with a brief prayer aloud. Use what you've learned in the lesson as a springboard to worship. For instance, praise God for His active participation in the lives of His people, even ordinary people like Naomi, Ruth, and Boaz. Thank Him for not giving up on His people in the depraved time of the judges. Thank Him for participating in your lives. Then share any specific prayer requests, and take time to pray for each group member to understand and apply the book of Ruth.

1. *The NIV Study Bible,* edited by Kenneth Barker (Grand Rapids, Michigan: Zondervan Corporation, 1985), page 353.
2. Second Samuel 5:4; J. I. Packer, Merrill C. Tenney, and William White, Jr., *The World of the Old Testament* (Nashville: Thomas Nelson Publishers, 1982), page 43.
3. Leon Morris, *Ruth: an Introduction and Commentary* (Downers Grove, Illinois: InterVarsity Press, 1968), pages 229-239; *The NIV Study Bible,* page 363. Morris' commentary is published together with *Judges: an Introduction and Commentary* by Arthur E. Cundall in the Tyndale Old Testament Commentary Series.
4. Gordon Fee and Douglas Stuart, *How to Read the Bible for All Its Worth* (Grand Rapids, Michigan: Zondervan Corporation, 1982), page 78.

RUTH 1:1-22

Naomi and Ruth Return

Have you ever felt that God is against you because your world is crumbling around you? As you read 1:1-22 again, put yourself first in Naomi's and then in Ruth's place.

Naomi emptied

For Further Study:
What else does Scripture say about Bethlehem? See 1 Samuel 16:1, Micah 5:2-5, Matthew 2:1-6, Luke 2:1-7.

Famine (1:1). Israel depended on unreliable rainfall for fertility, so drought and famine were common. Because of odd wind patterns, there could be famine in Judah and adequate rain just across the Dead Sea in Moab.[1]

Bethlehem in Judah (1:1). *Beth-lechem* meant "house of bread"—probably "granary," a reference to the land's fertility for grain crops.[2] Olives and grapes were the chief produce of northern Israel, but Judah was a region of wheat and barley farmers.

     The House of Bread was empty of bread, so Naomi and family left.

Ephrathites (1:2). Ephrath was the old name for Bethlehem, and the surrounding region retained the name. The name may also have been used to distinguish "old-established families" from newer ones.[3]

Sons . . . husband (1:5). In that culture, a woman's worth and security depended on family. Wage

21

work essentially did not exist for a woman, and she couldn't cultivate land without male relatives even if she were allowed to inherit it. (Naomi held the family land at Bethlehem— 4:3—but it was useless to her.) So, her only hope of livelihood was managing the household and raising the children of a husband. She needed sons, not daughters, because grown sons would support her if her husband died. Also, bearing sons was a woman's mission in life; barrenness was regarded as a disgrace and divine curse. Therefore, a childless widow too old to remarry was both worthless and vulnerable.[4]

Study Skill—Names in Scripture
To the Hebrew mind, a person's name represented his character and foretold something about his life. Names of biblical characters often, but not always, have some symbolic meaning.

Elimelech . . . Naomi (1:2). The names mean "(My) God is King" and "Pleasant, lovely, delightful." Both are good Hebrew names, and both reflect themes of the book.[5]

Mahlon . . . Kilion (1:2). These are old Canaanite (pagan) names meaning "weak" and "pining" (or "annihilation").[6]

Ruth (1:4). We don't know what her name meant in the language of Moab, but it sounds like the Hebrew for "friendship."[7]

1. Describe Naomi's condition after ten years in Moab (1:1-5).

Optional Application: Have you ever felt empty and afflicted by God as Naomi did? How did you respond? What did God do in your situation?

2. How does Naomi herself describe her situation (1:20-21)?

_____

_____

_____

_____

_____

3. To what does Naomi attribute her plight (1:13,20-21)?

_____

_____

_____

_____

Almighty (1:20-21). The exact meaning of the word *Shaddai* is debated, but it may mean "the Mountain One" and probably suggests unlimited power.[8]

4. Put yourself in Naomi's place. How would you feel? What would you do? How would you feel about and talk to God?

_____

_____

_____

_____

For Thought and Discussion: To what extent was Naomi's view of God's hand in her life accurate (1:13,20-21)?

For Further Study: In a concordance, look up references to God "visiting" people. (This is the KJV and NASB translation. The NIV uses various renderings.) What do you learn about God?

Optional Application: Think about God's names: *Shaddai* and *Yahweh*—the Almighty and the I AM PRESENT. What difference do these aspects of Him make to your life?

5. How should a Christian respond to this kind of tragedy? (*Optional:* See Psalms 13, 86; 2 Corinthians 1:8-11, 4:7-18, 5:1-10, 12:7-10.)

_____

_____

_____

_____

_____

_____

_____

_____

_____

Ruth and Orpah choose

Come to the aid of (1:6). Literally, "visited." In the Old Testament it is always a momentous occasion for good or ill when the Lord visits.

Mother's home (1:8). Ancient writers usually referred to the father's home, but this book was written from a woman's point of view. Likewise, it was unusual to speak of a man as some woman's husband (1:3).[9]

LORD (1:8). The personal name of Israel's God was written *YHWH*, for vowels were not written in Hebrew. It may have been pronounced "Yahweh," but the Jews came to regard it as too holy to be spoken, so the pronunciation has been forgotten. Most English Bibles render the divine name as "the LORD" in capitals. The name means "I AM WHO I AM" (Exodus 3:14)—the God who *is actively present* with His people.[10]

Naomi invokes her Israelite God by name to bless her Moabite daughters-in-law, rather than just invoking "God" in general or "Chemosh," the god of Moab. For Naomi, there is only one God.[11]

Show kindness (1:8). The word *hesed* means love, kindness, loyalty, faithfulness, constancy, commitment. It is the attitude and behavior between persons bound by a covenant or family ties. It is one of the Lord's chief traits toward Israel. (See Psalm 17:7, 42:8; Jeremiah 31:3. Or, look up *lovingkindness* and *mercy* in a concordance.) The same word is used in 2:20 and 3:10.

Rest (1:9). This key Old Testament idea includes peace, security, and blessing. God promised it to Israel if the people remained loyal to Him, but the nation enjoyed it only briefly under Joshua and again under David and Solomon (Deuteronomy 3:19-20, 12:8-10; Joshua 1:13, 21:43-22:8; 1 Kings 5:4). The book of Hebrews says that the Kingdom of God is the fulfillment of the Sabbath-rest promised to Israel (Hebrews 3:7-4:11).

Here in Ruth, Naomi is speaking of the security and blessing a woman could attain only if she was married, but a Hebrew reader could not miss the allusion to the rest Israel longed for.

Sons, who could become your husbands (1:11). The Law stated that if a man died, his brother had to marry the widow to protect her and perpetuate the family name (Deuteronomy 25:5-10, Mark 12:18-27). This is called *levirate* marriage from the Latin word *levir*, "brother-in-law." (The levirate was extended to include other kin when there was no brother, as Ruth 4 illustrates.)

Her people and her gods (1:15). The tie to kin and ancestral gods was strong, and the fear of strangers and strange gods was natural. Furthermore, Orpah knew that her chances of remarriage in Judah were slim. Israelites were prejudiced against foreigners, and the children of a Moabite might be barred from the religious congregation (Deuteronomy 23:3-6). A man

For Thought and Discussion: Ruth and Orpah could find rest only in marriage. How was Israel's position similar? How is the Church's position similar?

For Further Study: Trace the promise of rest in Scripture. What does it mean, and what does it mean for your life? How can you enter God's rest?

Optional Application: Put yourself in Ruth's place. What would be the sensible thing to do? What would be the loving thing to do? What would you do? Why?

Optional Application: Do you know anyone who is hurting as Naomi was (1:13,20-21)? If so, how can you show commitment like Ruth's toward that person? What will such commitment cost you?

For Thought and Discussion: How does Jesus treat you as Ruth treated Naomi?

would prefer an Israelite virgin to a penniless Moabite widow.

6. Both Ruth and Orpah originally planned to stay with Naomi (1:10). What priorities and considerations persuaded Orpah to return to her mother's house (1:8-9,11-13)?

_____

_____

_____

_____

_____

_____

_____

7. What does Ruth's choice tell you about her (1:6-17)?

_____

_____

_____

_____

_____

_____

May the LORD (1:17). Ruth invokes a solemn curse on herself if she breaks her word. This form of oath was probably accompanied by an illustrative gesture as the person said, "May the Lord do _so_ to me if. . . ."[12]
     Notice that Ruth invokes Yahweh.

8. a. How do Jesus and Paul describe love in the following verses?

John 15:13 _____

_____

_____

Philippians 2:4 _____

_____

_____

b. How does Ruth exemplify this kind of love in Ruth 1:16-17?

_____

_____

_____

_____

_____

_____

_____

9. Consider what Ruth was risking to stay with Naomi. How can you show this kind of self-less love toward someone?

_____

_____

_____

_____

_____

_____

_____

10. What would you be risking by doing this?

_____

_____

For Thought and Discussion: Ruth 1:16-17 is often quoted at weddings, but Ruth addressed it to her mother-in-law. Is this surprising? Why or why not? Can you imagine saying this to your mother-in-law, if you have one?

Optional Application: Meditate on 1:16-17. (You might memorize it.) Do you have this kind of commitment to anyone? If so, how can you act on it? If not, what hinders you from this type of commitment? What can you do to have your heart and actions transformed?

_____

_____

Study Skill—Application

It can be helpful to plan an application in five steps:

1. Record the verse or passage that contains the truth you want to apply to your life. If the passage is short enough, consider copying it word for word, as an aid to memory. For instance:

"Ruth remains loyal to Naomi, accompanying her to Bethlehem even though she may be giving up her chance for a husband and security (1:16-17)."

2. State the truth of the passage that is relevant to you. For example:

"Ruth's loyalty reflects the selfless love for other people that I should have."

3. Tell how you fall short in relation to this truth, like this:

"I tend to do what seems best, safest, or most fulfilling for me, rather than what would be best for those around me. I can't remember the last time I risked my own happiness for someone else."

4. State one specific thing you can do toward having your life changed in this area. (Ask God what, if anything, you can do. Don't forget that transformation depends on His will, power, and timing, not on yours. Diligent prayer should always be part of your application.) For instance:

"It will cost us money and effort to have my husband's mother live with us now that she is unable to live alone, but living with us will be better for her than living in a nursing home. I'm going to pray every day for the next week that God will enable me to rejoice in this decision and make her feel welcome."

5. If you tend to forget applications, plan a way to remind yourself to do what you have decided, such as putting a note on your refrigerator or in your office.[13]

28

11. If there is some other aspect of this chapter that you would like to apply to yourself, write it down along with your plans for prayer and meditation.

_____

_____

_____

_____

_____

_____

Optional Application: Ask the Lord to send you someone like Naomi to love, or to give you love like Ruth's for someone.

12. If you have any questions about 1:1-22 or the information in this lesson, write them here.

_____

_____

_____

_____

For the group

There is a lot of meat in this lesson. Feel free to take more than one meeting to discuss it if you have time.

Worship.

Warm-up. A simple question that deals generally with the topic of the study but focuses on people's experience can help the group shift from the day's affairs to Bible study. You can either discuss the warm-up question or just think about it for a minute in silence. A possible warm-up for this lesson is, "What is the worst tragedy you have ever experienced in your life?" This should help you identify with Naomi, since childless widowhood was about the worst thing that could happen to a woman in that society.

Read aloud. Even when the group has studied the passage ahead of time, most people will be glad to

29

have their memories refreshed. So, have someone read 1:1-22 aloud.

Summarize. A quick summary at the outset helps to set the context for the rest of the discussion. Briefly, what is 1:1-22 about? What events take place?

Questions. Give everyone a chance to ask questions about what happens and about the background material in this lesson. It's wise to clear up any confusion as soon as possible.

Naomi. Questions 1-5 try to help you first understand, then identify with, and then evaluate Naomi's situation and her response to it. You could ask one or two members of the group to come prepared to act out what they would say to God in Naomi's place (question 4).

To apply the scene to yourselves, consider what you and your situations have in common with Naomi and hers. For instance, Naomi was left, bereft, and empty; are you in any way left, bereft, or empty? Naomi attributed her suffering to God; was she right to do this? Why or why not? Should you attribute your sufferings to God? How should suffering affect a person's attitude toward God?

If any group members are feeling bereft and empty as Naomi did, you might plan time at the end of your meeting to pray for those people.

Ruth and Orpah. Questions 6-10 help you identify with and evaluate Ruth and Orpah. Again, for application, look for ways in which your situation resembles theirs. What choices are facing you? Are any of them like Ruth's?

Ask group members what they think of the Study Skill on page 28, and have someone share his or her answers to question 11. Is this method of planning an application helpful? Why or why not? You may want to go over the method step by step if it is new to the group.

Pray for any group member who is struggling to act like Ruth in some situation.

Summarize. To help everyone's memories, briefly summarize what you learned from 1:1-22 and some of the ways you plan to apply it.

Worship. Praise God for staying with Naomi in the midst of her suffering and bitterness, and for sending her Ruth as the living witness of His love. Thank Him for the ways He shows that He is with you. Ask Him to enable each of you to face sorrows and to be like Ruth for others.

1. Morris, page 246.
2. Morris, page 248.
3. Morris, page 249.
4. Roland de Vaux, *Ancient Israel: Volume 1: Social Institutions* (New York: McGraw-Hill Book Company, 1965), pages 39-41, 54; Morris, page 255.
5. *The NIV Study Bible,* page 365; Morris, page 249.
6. Morris, page 249.
7. *The NIV Study Bible,* page 365.
8. Morris, pages 264-268; *The NIV Study Bible,* page 30.
9. Morris, page 250-253.
10. J. A. Motyer, "The Names of God," *Eerdmans' Handbook to the Bible*, edited by David Alexander and Pat Alexander (Grand Rapids, Michigan: William B. Eerdmans Publishing Company, 1973), page 157.
11. Morris, pages 253-254.
12. Morris, page 261.
13. This "Five-point Application" is based on the method in *The 2:7 Series*, Course 4 (Colorado Springs, Colorado: NavPress, 1979), pages 50-51.

RUTH 2:1-3:18

Ruth and Boaz

The Lord brought Naomi back to Bethlehem empty and afflicted (1:21). But just as He sent rain to refill the House of Bread with grain at harvest time, so He was about to end the famine in Naomi's life. Read 2:1-3:18, observing how God accomplished His merciful plan.

Study Skill—Interpreting and Applying Old Testament Narratives

Gordon Fee and Douglas Stuart offer these principles to keep in mind:

1. "An Old Testament narrative usually does not directly teach a doctrine."

2. "An Old Testament narrative usually illustrates a doctrine or doctrines taught propostionally elsewhere." (There are no commands to us in Ruth, only examples to follow or not follow. There is little direct teaching about God; we learn about Him from observing the events.)

3. "*All* narratives are selective and incomplete. Not all the relevant details are always given (compare John 21:25). What does appear in the narrative is everything that the inspired author thought important for us to know."

4. "Narratives are not written to answer all our theological questions. They have particular, specific limited purposes and deal

(continued on page 34)

(continued from page 33)
with certain issues, leaving others to be dealt
with elsewhere, in other ways."
   5. "Narratives may teach either explicitly
(by clearly stating something) or implicitly (by
clearly implying something without actually
stating it)." Ruth 3:10 tells us explicitly that
Ruth has been showing "kindness"; the ear-
lier part of the story shows implicitly how she
has been kind if we understand the customs
and duties of that time. But *implicit* does not
mean *hidden*; beware of teachers who find
insights hidden in a book that most Bible
students cannot see.
   6. "In the final analysis, God is the hero
of all biblical narratives."[1]

Meeting in the harvest field (2:1-23)

Barley harvest (1:22). Barley was harvested in late
   April through early May; the wheat harvest
   (2:23) followed in May and early June.
      Harvesting grain involved these steps: "(1)
   cutting the ripened standing grain with hand
   sickles . . . usually done by men; (2) binding
   the grain into sheaves—usually done by
   women; (3) gleaning, i.e., gathering stalks of
   grain left behind (2:7); (4) transporting the
   sheaves to the threshing floor—often by don-
   key, sometimes by cart . . . ; (5) threshing, i.e.,
   loosening the grain from the straw—usually
   done by the treading of cattle . . . but sometimes by toothed threshing sledges . . . or the
   wheels of carts . . . ; (6) winnowing—done by
   tossing the grain into the air with winnowing
   forks . . . so that the wind, which usually came
   up for a few hours in the afternoon, blew away
   the straw and chaff . . . leaving the grain at the
   winnower's feet; (7) sifting the grain . . . to
   remove any residual foreign matter; (8) bagging
   for transportation and storage."[2]

Pick up the leftover grain (2:2). The Law required
   landowners to leave the grain at the edges of
   their fields and any ears that the harvesters

dropped. The poor, aliens, widows, and father-less were supposed to be allowed to **glean** (2:3) those leftovers for their own needs (Deuteron-omy 24:19). This system provided for the poor but let them work for their needs rather than depending upon outright charity.

Ruth planned to glean **behind anyone in whose eyes I find favor** (2:2). She may not have known that in Israel gleaning was a right, not a special privilege. Or, she may have known that not all landowners respected God's Law since there was no one to enforce it.

I have told the men not to touch you (2:9). The ideal position for a gleaner was right behind the harvesters, where one would be the first to pick up whatever stalks fell from the sheaves. How-ever, a gleaner who followed too closely might be repulsed by the workmen defending the crop, and a defenseless woman among strange men was vulnerable to obscene remarks and even rough handling.[3]

1. A single woman had few ways to support herself in those days. She could beg, sell herself into slavery, become a prostitute, look for a husband among the eligible men of the village, or seek support from her nearest male relative. Or, during the two months of harvest, she could glean.

Consider the risks of gleaning and the alternatives facing Ruth and Naomi. What do you learn about Ruth from the fact that she undertook to glean to support both herself and her mother-in-law?

_____

_____

_____

_____

_____

_____

2. What else do the following verses reveal about Ruth's character?

2:7 _____

_____

_____

2:10,13 _____

_____

_____

_____

Water jars (2:9). "Gleaning in the heat of harvesttime would be thirsty work, and no doubt the water so laboriously drawn and carried to the place of reaping would be jealously guarded from all but those entitled to make use of it. Valuable time would be lost if a gleaner had to draw her own water,"[4] for the well was probably far from the fields.

The law of gleaning did not require the landowner to provide either food or water or protection from the men.

---

3. What do the following verses tell about Boaz?

2:4 _____

_____

_____

2:11-12 _____

_____

_____

_____

2:8-9,14-16 _____

_____

36

_____

_____

_____

Optional Application: Meditate on 2:20a. How can you show kindness to the living and the dead as Boaz did?

Threshed (2:17). A small amount of grain could be threshed by beating it with a club.[5]

Ephah (2:17). About four gallons, a large amount for a gleaner.

Kinsman-redeemers (2:20). The Hebrew word *go'el* recurs in 3:9,12,13 and 4:1,3,6,8,14; it is a key word in the story. The verb means "to redeem" or "to act as a kinsman." The noun means "kinsman," but it implies the duties that went with blood relationship.

    "The kinsman-redeemer was responsible for protecting the interests of needy members of the extended family—e.g., to provide an heir for a brother who had died (Deuteronomy 25:5-10), to redeem land that a poor relative had sold outside the family (Leviticus 25:25-28), to redeem a relative who had been sold into slavery [for debts] (Leviticus 25:47-49) and to avenge the killing of a relative (Numbers 35:19-21; 'avenger' and 'kinsman-redeemer' are translations of the same Hebrew word)."[6]

For Further Study: Look up other references to the *go'el*—Job 19:25; Psalm 19:14, 78:35; Jeremiah 50:34; and the many references to the "Redeemer" in Isaiah.

Meeting at the threshing floor (3:1-18)

In chapter 2, Ruth took the initiative to provide for Naomi. For perhaps a month, Ruth gleaned daily in Boaz's field. Every day she joined the hired laborers for the midday meal. She saw how Boaz supervised his workers, and he saw her diligent labor and virtuous behavior. Perhaps the two even spoke together occasionally.

    But now both barley and wheat harvests are over, and it is time for threshing and winnowing. There is no more gleaning and no hired work available for a woman, so Ruth can only stay home and consume her small store of grain. Boaz knows he is Elimelech's kinsman, yet he has done nothing to redeem his kinsman's land or posterity. Neither Naomi nor Ruth knows why; perhaps he is waiting because technically Naomi is the widow with first

For Thought and Discussion: How has Christ acted as your kinsman-redeemer?

Optional Application: How does James describe true religion and living faith in James 1:27 and 2:1-17? Did Boaz live up to this standard? How can you apply this teaching?

Optional Application: Is there someone other than a family member toward whom you could show active kindness like Boaz's? Pray about this.

claim on the *go'el*. So to bring matters to a head, Naomi takes the initiative to provide for Ruth, formally waiving her own right to marry the *go'el*.

4. In 2:20, Naomi praises Boaz for his "kindness," using the same word as in 1:8—covenant love, commitment, loyalty. How has Boaz already shown the loyal kindness of a kinsman to "the dead" (2:20)? See 2:8-16.

_____

_____

_____

_____

5. How does Boaz show the kindness of a kinsman-redeemer in 3:10-15?

_____

_____

_____

_____

_____

6. In 3:10, Boaz praises Ruth for her "kindness" in seeking a middle-aged husband from Elime-lech's family rather than a young husband from another family. Toward whom is Ruth showing loyalty and love by doing this? How is Ruth's choice an act of kindness? (See 1:11; 4:5,10, 13-17. See also the notes on pages 25 and 37.)

_____

_____

_____

_____

_____

7. For what kindness did Boaz commend Ruth in 2:11-12?

_____

_____

_____

_____

8. Judges 21:25 says, "In those days Israel had no king; everyone did as he saw fit"—that is, because people did not acknowledge God as their King and had no human king, they did what pleased themselves. How were Ruth and Boaz different from most people?

_____

_____

_____

_____

9. To what extent are Ruth's, Boaz's, and Naomi's attitudes toward family applicable to us? Why? State some principles for Christian family duty. (*Optional:* Consider Genesis 2:24; Matthew 15:1-9; Luke 9:59-62, 14:26, 18:29-30; Ephesians 6:1-4; 1 Timothy 5:8,16.)

_____

_____

_____

_____

_____

_____

_____

For Thought and Discussion: Should a Christian do as he or she sees fit? What should govern a Christian's actions? See John 15:9-14 and Philippians 2:1-8.

Optional Application: Do you tend to do as you see fit? How can you follow Ruth's and Boaz's example in this area?

For Thought and Discussion: Why do you think loyalty toward family members was so important to these people?

For Thought and Discussion: How does Naomi show kindness to Ruth (3:1-4)?

For Thought and Discussion: How do you suppose the whole town came to recognize Ruth's noble character during the two months she had been in Bethlehem (3:11)?

A home (3:1). Literally, "rest" as in 1:9.

Threshing floor (3:3). This was probably a space of hard, smooth rock or clay in an exposed place downwind of the village. It had to be carefully chosen to catch the afternoon or evening breeze, since both threshing and winnowing were done there.

Once the work was done, the men stayed to eat, drink, and dance, but the women went home. The landowner stayed the whole night to guard the grain from theft.[7]

Uncover his feet and lie down (3:4). This custom is not mentioned elsewhere in ancient writings, but the context makes clear that it is a request for marriage. Boaz does not think it promiscuous (3:11). Ancient people used garments symbolically in many ways. Among the Arabs to *spread the corner of your garment over* (3:9) a woman was to take her in marriage, so 3:9 is definitely a proposal.[8] Thus, in 3:7 Ruth simply acts out the request she makes verbally in 3:9.

The corner of your garment (3:9) is literally "your skirt" or "your wings," to remind us of 2:12. The wings of a husband's long robe around his wife symbolized the protective rest he gave her. By consenting to Ruth's request (3:9), Boaz would fulfill his own prayer for her (2:12).

Although we assume that what Naomi told Ruth to do (3:4) was customary, there was certainly a risk involved in sending a pretty girl to lie down in an isolated place next to a man who had been drinking heavily. Boaz's behavior says something about him.

Woman of noble character (3:11). "Woman of worth" in RSV; "woman of excellence" in NASB; "virtuous woman" in KJV. This is not limited to chastity, but "denotes ability or efficiency or attainment in any one of a number of directions."[9]

The Hebrew for "of noble character" is translated "of standing" ("of wealth" in KJV) in 2:1. Both Ruth and Boaz are noted for their loyal kindness and their noble excellence.

The goal in application is not merely to obey just this once, but to be "transformed by the renewing of your mind" (Romans 12:2), "to put on the new self, created to be like God in true righteousness and holiness" (Ephesians 4:24). God intends us "to be conformed to the likeness of his Son" (Romans 8:29). Therefore, the aim of every application should be to make Christlike attitudes and behavior a habit. Because the breaking of old habits and establishing of godly ones requires time and God's help, you may sometimes need to concentrate on application in the same area of your life for several weeks. You may decide to pray daily for God to root a particular character quality in you and to show you opportunities to practice it. As an aid to prayer, you can keep a record of how you respond to each opportunity. You may need to confess failure often as you grow, but the focused attention will help you see God at work in your life.

Optional Application: Do you have a noble character? How do your current circumstances give you an opportunity to display it?

For Further Study: Study the attributes of a noble (excellent, worthy) woman in Proverbs 31.

10. a. What one example or lesson from 2:1-3:18 would you like to apply to your own life?

_____

_____

_____

_____

_____

   b. How do you fall short in this area, or how would you like to grow?

_____

_____

_____

_____

_____

Optional Application: How can you act with kindness or loyalty toward someone—a family member or someone else?

For Further Study: Describe the example of kindness or covenant love Jesus gives in Luke 10:25-37.

c. What prayer and/or action can you pursue during the next week or so to put this example into practice and develop it as a habit?

_____

_____

_____

_____

_____

_____

_____

d. Is there anything you plan to do to remind yourself? If so, what?

_____

_____

_____

_____

11. List any questions you have about 2:1-3:18.

_____

_____

_____

_____

For the group

Warm-up. Ask the group what *kindness* means to each of you. You might have several people give examples. When you discuss questions 4-9, consider whether the English word *kindness* expresses the meaning in 1:8, 2:20, and 3:10.

Read aloud. It may be more interesting if different people read each scene, or if you assign the words of Naomi, Ruth, Boaz, and the narrator to different people.

Summarize. What is 2:1-23 about? What is 3:1-18 about?

Questions. Most of the questions in this lesson ask you to describe Ruth's and Boaz's characters based on what they say and do. You have to interpret the *implicit* clues in the story to get the point. This may be hard for those who haven't studied many narratives, but really you've interpreted implicit clues anytime you've read a novel.

The key to good interpretation is thorough observation with the question, "What does this imply?" always in mind. For example, Ruth went to work in the fields of strangers in an unfamiliar culture at a time when Israel was lax with regard to justice and kindness. What does this show about Ruth? Similarly, in a time when most of Israel was flirting with Canaanite gods, the people in this story invoke, pray to, and even greet each other in the name of the Lord (1:8,17; 2:4,12,20; 3:10). Both Naomi and Boaz knew that Ruth could be in danger in other people's fields (2:8-9,22); perhaps not everyone was as obedient to God's Law as Boaz. What do his other actions toward Ruth (urging her to stay in his field, providing her with food and water, instructing the reapers to respect her and sneak her extra grain, not molesting her at the threshing floor, promising to either arrange her marriage or marry her himself, giving her six measures of barley) tell about him?

Two concepts are fundamental to understanding this story but are unfamiliar to us: the "kinsman-redeemer" (*go'el*) and "kindness" (*hesed*). In particular, the kinsman's duty to marry the widow in order to raise up children for the deceased seems strange to many modern people. But it is this "kindness" or loyalty that both Ruth and Boaz show toward Naomi, Elimelech, and Mahlon that is the focus of the story. Naomi praises Boaz for treating his kin's widow with kindness (2:20), Boaz praises Ruth for showing her dead husband and his mother kindness by marrying his kin (3:10), and Boaz shows kindness to his kin by acting as *go'el*, by accepting Ruth's proposal.

Once your group understands the family commitments that Ruth, Boaz, and Naomi take so seriously, it is up to you to decide how all this applies to you. Our culture does not take family as

43

seriously as those people, but what should Christians do?

Family responsibility needn't be your only topic of discussion. You might consider the phrase "woman of noble character" (3:11) or "man of standing" (2:1). How can you become men and women of excellence? Or, how can you show "kindness" to people outside your families?

Summarize. What has happened in the story so far? What is the story about? How do chapters 2 and 3 apply to you?

Wrap-up.

Worship. Thank God for people like Naomi, Ruth, and Boaz in the midst of corrupt generations. Pray that you may be like them. What other prayers and praises does this story prompt you to make?

1. Fee and Stuart, page 78.
2. *The NIV Study Bible,* page 366.
3. Morris, page 275.
4. Morris, page 275.
5. *The NIV Study Bible,* page 367.
6. *The NIV Study Bible,* page 367. See also Morris, pages 282-283; and de Vaux, pages 21-22.
7. *The NIV Study Bible,* pages 366,368; Morris, page 285.
8. Morris, pages 286-287,289; *The NIV Study Bible,* page 368.
9. Morris, page 291.

RUTH 4:1-22

Naomi Filled

Ruth took action in chapter 2; Naomi acted in chapter 3; now it is Boaz's turn. Read 4:1-22, observing the results of redemption.

Town gate (4:1). Towns of that time were built tightly with no open squares or forums. Therefore, public business was done in the open space before the gate. The city elders and other men could always be found there to adjudicate disputes and to witness legal and business transactions.[1]

Elders (4:2). These were the local judges (Joshua 20:4; 1 Kings 21:8,11).

Naomi . . . is selling the piece of land (4:3). This is the first we have heard of this property; apparently, the story leaves out some conversation in which Naomi told Boaz of her intent to sell. There may have been quite a bit of contact between Boaz and the women during the past two months.

Technically, widows could not inherit their husbands' property (Numbers 27:8-11).[2] However, since in this case Elimelech had no children, brothers, or uncles, the community apparently gave Naomi the right to dispose of the land.[3] Because she couldn't farm it herself, she had to sell it, and buying it was part of the go'el's obligation to Elimelech.

45

For Thought and Discussion: a. Why was it important that the name of the dead man should not disappear from the family or be separated from his property (4:5,10)?

b. What does this show about Israel's view of family and property?

c. Christians don't practice the customs of raising children and redeeming property in someone else's name. Why not?

Endanger my own estate (4:6). Boaz has presented the unnamed kinsman with a dual responsibility: if he agrees to act as *go'el,* he must pay both to buy Elimelech's land and to support Mahlon's widow. If the kinsman could buy the land without Ruth, then the land would become part of his estate and would pass to his sons in his name. However, if he marries Ruth, then her first son and the land are both reckoned as Mahlon's. In that case, the kinsman will have paid Naomi for the land and paid to support Ruth and her son, but none of that expense will be credited to his estate. Worse yet, if he has only one son, then all his property will be inherited in Mahlon's name. In order *to maintain the name of the dead with his property* (4:5), the kinsman will have risked having his own name lost.

The kinsman might also endanger his own estate by marrying a Moabitess; notice that Boaz reminds everyone of Ruth's origin in 4:5.

Took off his sandal (4:7). This was how the kinsman transferred to Boaz his right to Mahlon's land and widow.

1. Think about the choices Boaz and the unnamed kinsman each make in 4:2-10. What do you learn about each man's priorities?

the unnamed kinsman _____

_____

_____

_____

_____

Boaz _____

_____

_____

_____

_____

46

2. Why is it fitting that no name is recorded for the kinsman who declined to be the *go'el* for his family (4:5-6,10)?

_____

_____

_____

_____

_____

Optional Application: Buying the land and marrying Ruth was an expensive and risky undertaking. Are you faced with any similar decision? If so, how can you follow Boaz's example in the priorities you choose?

3. How was Boaz rewarded for risking his own name and posterity (Ruth 4:18-22, Matthew 1:5-16)?

_____

_____

_____

_____

_____

4. Can we draw any conclusions from questions 1-3 that are relevant to us? If so, what?

_____

_____

_____

_____

_____

_____

5. How did Ruth and Boaz's marriage affect Naomi? (Compare 1:5,21 to 4:13-17.)

_____

_____

_____

_____

47

For Thought and Discussion: Why is it significant that God did not intervene in Naomi's life with blatant miracles and appearances?

Optional Application: Does God act in your life as He did in Naomi's? If so, how? How should this lead you to respond?

6. Remember what Naomi thought God was doing in her life when she was empty of wealth, family, and status (1:13,20-21). What part did God play in filling her emptiness? (See 2:3,12; 3:11; 4:13.)

_____

_____

_____

_____

_____

_____

7. You wrote in question 5 how the faithful acts of Ruth and Boaz contributed to God's plan to restore Naomi's fullness. How did their faithfulness serve God's will for . . .

Elimelech and Mahlon (4:10)? _____

_____

_____

_____

the nation of Israel (4:18-22)? _____

_____

_____

_____

8. What does the story of Ruth show about God's responsibility and people's responsibility in working out God's plans?

God's responsibility _____

_____

_____

_____

people's responsibility _____

_____

_____

_____

Optional
Application: Does
God act in your life as
He did in Naomi's? If
so, how? How should
this lead you to
respond?

9. Read the old covenant law of Deuteronomy 23:3 and the promise of the new covenant in Isaiah 56:3-8. Why is it significant that David and Jesus were descended from a Moabitess?

_____

_____

_____

_____

_____

10. a. Is there one insight from this lesson that you would like to take to heart? If so, write it down. (Consider the Optional Applications in the margins.)

_____

_____

_____

_____

b. How would you like this insight to affect the way you treat God or other people?

_____

_____

_____

_____

_____

_____

49

Optional Application: Could your parents or in-laws say that you are better to them than seven sons? What does this kind of praise say about how a person like Ruth treats her family? How can you be like this?

c. What steps—including prayer and action—can you take to begin to grow in this area?

_____

_____

_____

_____

_____

_____

_____

Like Rachel and Leah (4:11). As these women built up the house of Jacob-Israel by bearing the fathers of the twelve tribes (Genesis 30), so Ruth built up the house of Israel by bearing the grandfather of David. Israel was in a sorry state until David became king. Also, God promised "to 'build' the house of David as an enduring dynasty, through which Israel's blessed destiny would be assured (see 2 Samuel 7:27-29)."[4]

Perez (4:12). He was the father of the most prominent clan of Judah, the one to which Boaz belonged. Perez was the son of a levirate union between a man and his daughter-in-law (Genesis 38:27-30), just as Ruth and Boaz's marriage followed the levirate custom.

This blessing was also fulfilled. As the clan of Perez was the greatest in Judah, so the family of Obed became the greatest in Judah (and even in all Israel) because of David.

Kinsman-redeemer (4:14). The baby Obed is Naomi's *go'el* because through him she will have descendants and he will support her if Boaz dies.

Better to you than seven sons (4:15). "Since seven was considered a number of completeness, to have seven sons was the epitome of all family blessings in Israel (see 1 Samuel 2:5; Job 1:2; 42:13)."[5]

50

11. List any questions you have about the material
in this lesson.

_____

_____

_____

_____

For the group

Warm-up. Ask everyone if it is important to him or
her to make a "name" for himself or herself.

Read aloud.

Summarize.

Questions. This lesson deals with man's and God's
responsibility for seeing that God's will is done.
Questions 1-4 contrast Boaz and the other kinsman:
Why did the one man fulfill his responsibility while
the other man declined to do so? What happened to
each man because of his choice? Is there a lesson
here for us?

Questions 5-9 look at God's will for Naomi, her
family, and all Israel. How did God and people work
together to fulfill His plans? Did the people need to
know all about the plans? What did they need to
know, and why? How is all this relevant to the decisions facing you?

Finally, question 10 asks you to apply what
you've learned about God's involvement and human
responsibility.

Worship. Praise God for being present in Naomi's
and Ruth's lives to provide them with a redeemer,
even though things looked bleak for months. Thank
God for providing you with a Redeemer and rest.
Thank Him for people like Boaz. Ask Him to make
you more like Ruth and Boaz.

1. Morris, pages 297-298.
2. de Vaux, page 54.
3. Morris, pages 300-301.
4. *The NIV Study Bible,* page 369.
5. *The NIV Study Bible,* page 370.

REVIEW OF RUTH

The Redeemer

Types

Study Skill—Types in the Old Testament

A *type* is an Old Testament person, object, or event that God designed to resemble its *antitype*[1] in the New Testament. God gave types to prepare Israel to understand Christ, and to be moral and doctrinal examples for us (1 Corinthians 10:6,11; Hebrews 10:1). In some cases the New Testament explicitly states that something in the Old Testament is a type (Hebrews 7:3, 9:8-9, 11:19; 1 Peter 3:21). At other times it does not. Some interpreters have fallen into error by abusing typology, but we can avoid foolish mistakes if we keep some principles in mind.

1. "No doctrine or theory should ever be built upon a type or types independently of direct teaching elsewhere in Scripture." Types are meant to illustrate, amplify, and illuminate doctrines taught explicitly elsewhere.[2]

2. "The parallelism between type and antitype should not be pressed to fanciful extremes."[3] Boaz and Ruth may remind us in some ways of Christ and the Church, but they also differ in many ways from Christ and the Church.

(continued on page 54)

53

(continued from page 53)

3. Unless the New Testament explicitly says that an Old Testament narrative describes a type, we should study the narrative primarily for its plain meaning and be cautious in seeing types in it. We make tentative claims about typology in Ruth only after paying most attention to what the story means if the people are just people. Also, we don't try to make Naomi, Orpah, the unnamed kinsman, and the kinsman's sandal into types.

1. Read Isaiah 54:5 and Ezekiel 16:1-14. How do Boaz and Ruth resemble God and Israel?

_____

_____

_____

_____

_____

2. Read Ephesians 5:25-32 and Revelation 21:2,9-10. In what ways are Boaz and Ruth types of Christ and the Church?

_____

_____

_____

_____

_____

3. Review how Boaz acts as a kinsman-redeemer toward Ruth (2:8-9,11-12,14-16,20; 3:1, 10-13,15; 4:1-10). What does he do?

_____

_____

_____

_____

_____

_____

4. In what similar ways is Christ our kinsman-redeemer?

_____

_____

_____

_____

_____

_____

5. How does Ruth model the way we should act toward Christ (2:10,13; 3:9)?

_____

_____

_____

_____

_____

_____

6. Does this study of Ruth and Boaz as types suggest any applications to you (such as topics for prayer, actions, or decisions)? If so, write down your thoughts.

_____

_____

_____

_____

_____

_____

For Further Study:
How does the book of
Ruth illustrate the fol-
lowing scriptures:
Acts 10:24-35, Deuter-
onomy 10:17-18,
Isaiah 58:6-7?

Review

Now that you've studied the story in detail, it's time
to look at the book as a whole again. To remind
yourself of what you've studied, skim the story from
start to finish and reread your answers in lessons
one through four. Ask God to give you a firm grasp
of the key things He wants you to learn from Ruth.

7. Recall what "kindness" (1:8, 2:20, 3:10) means
   from pages 25 and 37. How do Naomi, Ruth,
   and Boaz show kindness to each other?

Naomi _____

_____

_____

_____

_____

Ruth _____

_____

_____

_____

_____

_____

Boaz _____

_____

_____

_____

_____

_____

8. What did you learn about God from this story?

_____

_____

_____

_____

_____

_____

9. In question 4 on page 16, you said what you
   thought the story was about after your first
   reading. What do you now think are its main
   themes or purposes?

_____

_____

_____

_____

_____

_____

_____

10. What are some of the key lessons for your own
    life that you have learned from studying Ruth?

_____

_____

_____

_____

_____

_____

57

11. Look back at questions in previous lessons in which you described some application you wanted to make.

a. Have you noticed any areas (thoughts, attitudes, opinions, behavior) in which you have changed as a result of studying Ruth? If so, how have you changed?

_____

_____

_____

_____

_____

_____

b. Ask God to show you any areas on which you still need to concentrate for growth. Write any thoughts or plans here.

_____

_____

_____

_____

_____

_____

_____

12. Review the questions you listed at the ends of lessons one through four. Do any important ones remain unanswered? If so, some of the sources on pages 117-121 may help you find answers, or you can ask someone for help. Write your questions here.

_____

_____

_____

_____

_____

_____

For the group

Warm-up. Ask group members what they thought
"redeemer" meant before studying Ruth.

Read aloud. It would be a good idea to read the
whole story again to refresh everyone's memory. If
this seems impossible, try reading 1:1-22 and 4:9-22.

Redeemer. Make sure that everyone understands
what a type is and why the principles in the Study
Skill are important. Technically, Ruth and Boaz are
types of the Church and Christ but symbols of Israel
and God, since a type is something that points to
the New Testament. How does the story of Ruth
help you understand Christ, our Redeemer?

Review. This section reviews both your interpretation and your application of the story. It's a chance
to get the main points clear in your minds, and also
to assess how well you've fulfilled your planned
applications. Give each person a chance to share
what he or she has learned and how he or she has
changed during the past five weeks. Also, let each
person share further plans for application.

    Some of you may think you haven't changed at
all. You may feel you don't understand application,
that circumstances kept you from doing what you
hoped, that you couldn't think of any ways in which
Ruth applies to you, or that you have a long way to
go before you are like Ruth and Boaz. Give everyone
a chance to share questions and frustrations, and
see if together you can solve any problems. How can
you help each other plan and carry out applications?
Can you commit yourselves to pray specifically for
the areas in which the others want to grow? Can
you see growth in each other that the other person
does not see in himself? This is a time to aid and
encourage each other, and to be aided and encouraged, not a time to prove how much better than

others you are at application.

Let group members raise questions about the book that remain unanswered. Then plan how you can work together to find the answers.

Evaluation. Take a few minutes to evaluate how your group functioned during your study of Ruth. Is there anything about your meetings that you would like to change when you study Esther? What aspects of your group are most and least helpful to each member? How well did you meet the goals you set at your first meeting? Will you go straight to Esther, or is there something else you want to do first?

Worship. Praise God for being your Redeemer and the Husband of the Church. Ask Him to help you and the whole Church be a more perfect Bride. Thank Him for Ruth's and Boaz's examples of kindness, and for all the other lessons you learned through this book.

1. The *antitype* is the New Testament person or thing fore-shadowed by the type. For instance, Boaz is a type of Christ, and Christ is the antitype of Boaz.
2. J. Sidlow Baxter, *Explore the Book* (Grand Rapids, Michigan: Zondervan Corporation, 1960), page 55.
3. Baxter, page 56.

OVERVIEW

The Story of Esther

Map of the Persian Empire

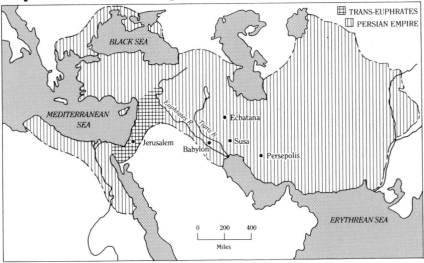

In Ruth we saw God at work in the lives of ordinary people when Israel was just a loose league of tribes in pagan Canaan. Only a century later, Ruth's great-grandson David led Israel to a pinnacle of fame, strength, and prosperity. Sadly, within another century the golden dream had faded like a mist as Israel split in two and plunged back into sin. Sin led to conquest by foreign empires, and the book of Esther finds the Jews scattered in pagan lands and threatened with extinction. Is God still in control? Is He still active in the lives of His people and working out His plans as He was in the days of Ruth, or has He finally abandoned Israel? The teller of Esther's tale tries to answer that question for his own generation.

61

TIMELINE FOR THE BOOK OF ESTHER

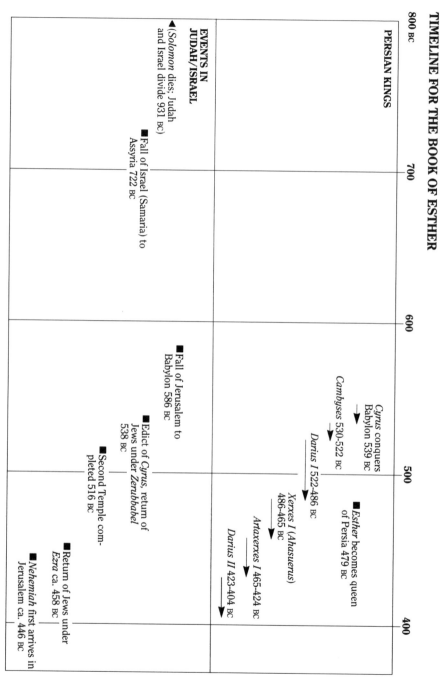

PERSIAN KINGS

800 BC — 700 — 600 — 500 — 400

Cyrus conquers Babylon 539 BC

Cambyses 530-522 BC

Darius I 522-486 BC

Xerxes I (Ahasuerus) 486-465 BC

Artaxerxes I 465-424 BC

Darius II 423-404 BC

■ Esther becomes queen of Persia 479 BC

EVENTS IN JUDAH/ISRAEL

▲ (Solomon dies; Judah and Israel divide 931 BC)

■ Fall of Israel (Samaria) to Assyria 722 BC

■ Fall of Jerusalem to Babylon 586 BC

■ Edict of Cyrus, return of Jews under Zerubbabel 538 BC

■ Second Temple completed 516 BC

■ Return of Jews under Ezra ca. 458 BC

■ Nehemiah first arrives in Jerusalem ca. 446 BC

Chronology of the Book of Esther

Xerxes I (Ahasuerus) becomes king	486 BC
Xerxes holds his banquet, deposes Vashti (Esther 1:3)	483
Persia fights Greece and is defeated	482-479
Esther becomes queen (Esther 2:16-17)	December 479-January 478
Haman plots against the Jews (Esther 3:7)	April-May 474
Xerxes issues the edict against the Jews (Esther 3:12)	April 17, 474
Xerxes issues the edict to protect the Jews (Esther 8:9)	June 25, 474
The day of destruction (Esther 3:13, 8:12)	March 7, 473
The first Purim celebration (Esther 9:17-19)	March 8-9, 473

Assyria, Babylon, Persia

When God made His covenant with Israel in the wilderness of Sinai, He promised to bless His people if they obeyed Him but to send them into exile if they were disloyal. Over and over the people rebelled, and God sent prophets to warn them. At last He allowed Assyria to destroy and deport the northern tribes of Israel in 722 BC. The southern tribe of Judah was spared then, and the people concluded that they were invincible because God was protecting them. But because they did not give up their sin, the unthinkable happened: God let Babylon smash Jerusalem and exile the Judahites.

The first exiles left Jerusalem in 605 BC with a promise that Babylon would rule for seventy years (Jeremiah 25:11-12). As prophesied (Isaiah 45:1-7), Cyrus of Persia defeated Babylon in 539 BC and instituted a new policy for his subjects: deported peoples could return to their native lands and rebuild temples to worship their native gods, so long as they remained loyal to Persia, paid their taxes, and offered prayers for Cyrus. Cyrus intended this merely as a shrewd way to cement an empire, but the effect was that the Jews were free to return to Judah.

However, fewer than 50,000 Jews actually did go to Judah in 538 BC (Ezra 2:64); perhaps ten times as many stayed in Babylonia, Persia, Egypt, and other places where they had settled. The many who had acquired property and businesses in pagan lands chose not to risk the journey to Judah, where fickle weather and hostile neighbors guaranteed poverty and hardship (see the books of Ezra, Nehemiah, Haggai, and Zechariah for the situation of the returned exiles).

Cyrus's son Cambyses was less friendly to the Jews than his father, but his successor Darius I finally agreed to finance the rebuilding of the Temple in Jerusalem. Construction had been halted from 536 to 520 BC because of opposition from the non-Jewish population of Palestine. Darius was tolerant of ethnic minorites as Cyrus had been, and he was also a superb leader. He solidified the Persian Empire from India to northern Sudan (Esther 1:1), improved administration, "introduced coinage, standardized weights and measures, and took an interest in the welfare of his subjects. But his new taxes were to cause the empire's downfall."[1]

Xerxes

Darius's son succeeded him on his death in 486 BC. *Xerxes* is the Greek version of this new king's Persian name, *Khshayarshan*. The book of Esther calls him *Ahasuerus*, which is the Hebrew version of this name.[2] (We will follow the NIV in using the Greek form, Xerxes, which in English is pronounced "Zerk-ceez.")

The Greek historian Herodotus, who was born around the time Xerxes took the throne, wrote a history of the wars between Greece and Persia. About a third of his book dealt with the reign of Xerxes. Herodotus described Xerxes as bold, ambitious, handsome, stately, and self-indulgent in every area. At one point, Xerxes was attracted to his brother Masistes' wife. When she rebuffed him, Xerxes first married her daughter Artaynte to his son Darius, then seduced Artaynte himself. Xerxes allowed his wife to take revenge on Artaynte's mother, and when Masistes fought back, Xerxes had his own brother and nephews killed along with their army.[3] This was the same king

> who ordered a bridge to be built over the Hellespont, and who, on learning that the bridge had been destroyed by a tempest, just after its completion, was so blindly enraged that he commanded three hundred strokes of the scourge to be inflicted on the sea, and a pair of fetters to be thrown into it at the Hel-

lespont, and then had the unhappy builders of the bridge beheaded. This is the king who, on being offered a sum equivalent to five and a half millions sterling [about $11,000,000] by Pythius, the Lydian, towards the expenses of a military expedition, was so enraptured at such loyalty that he returned the money, accompanied by a handsome present; and then, on being requested by this same Pythius, shortly afterwards, to spare him just one of his sons—the eldest—from the expedition, as the sole support of his declining years, furiously ordered the son to be cut into two pieces, and the army to march between them.[4]

In short, Herodotus's portrait of Xerxes is in perfect harmony with the character in the book of Esther, as incredible as the king's deeds may seem to us.

Persian chronicle?

Esther is one of the latest of the Old Testament books to be written. Its author is unknown, but he was almost certainly a Jew living in the Persian Empire, perhaps even Susa, for he had as accurate a knowledge of Persian customs and terms as modern archaeologists have. His description of the citadel of Susa was precise. He probably wrote after Xerxes' death in 465 BC, when such an unflattering portrait of the king would not have endangered either himself or Mordecai and Esther. He probably wrote before Alexander the Great conquered the Persian Empire in 331 BC, for he used Persian words frequently but never Greek ones.[5]

Esther has been called a historical short story (even an invented one)[6] and a wisdom tale written to illustrate the maxims of Proverbs. It was probably intended in part to be read liturgically at celebrations of the Jewish feast of Purim, which commemorates the events the book recounts. Recently, Robert Gordis has suggested that Esther may follow the style of an official Persian court chronicle, with legal phraseology (1:22, 3:12-14, 8:11-12) and careful lists of names (1:14, 9:7). The author writes objectively, calling Mordecai "the Jew" and his people "them" rather than "us."[7]

One of the author's favorite techniques was to

65

record duplications: three pairs of banquets, two lists of the king's servants (1:10,14), two reports that Esther concealed her identity (2:10,20), two gatherings of the women (2:8,19), two times when Mordecai is arrayed in royal robes (6:7-11, 8:15), two coverings of Haman's face (6:12, 7:8), and so on. There are other distinctive elements of the author's style, but you can observe them for yourself.

Purim

Most Christians are unfamiliar with the feast of Purim, but it is a favorite among Jews. In late February or early March, Jewish families gather to feast, give gifts, celebrate, and read the book of Esther aloud. Since the Jews have continued to be persecuted right up through this century, the book of Esther is dear to them.

Christians, however, have often not known what to do with the book. Martin Luther wrote of 2 Maccabees and Esther, "I wish that they did not exist at all; for they Judaize too much and have much heathen perverseness."[8] We'll leave it to you to decide what you think.

1. Read the whole book of Esther, observing the plot, characters, events or ideas that recur, and references to God. You can record your observations (questions 2-7) as you go along or afterward. But don't let taking notes keep you from enjoying the drama, humor, and suspense of this classic tale.

2. Feasting and celebrating recur through the book. Give a verse reference and brief description of each feast (banquet, celebration).

_____

_____

_____

_____

_____

_____

_____

_____

_____

_____

_____

_____

For Further Study:
Make a list of all the occurrences that are mentioned twice in the book.

3. Fasting occurs several times. Note each time fasting is mentioned, who fasts, and why.

    a. _____

    _____

    _____

    _____

    b. _____

    _____

    _____

    _____

    c. _____

    _____

    _____

    _____

4. Look for references to God and religious acts (such as prayer and worship). What do you find?

    _____

    _____

    _____

    _____

5. Briefly describe the main characters.

    Xerxes (Ahasuerus) _____

Haman _____

_____

_____

_____

Mordecai _____

_____

_____

_____

Esther _____

_____

_____

_____

6. To outline the plot of the story, make up a title
   for each episode.

   1:1-22 _____

   _____

   2:1-18 _____

   _____

   2:19-23 _____

   _____

   3:1-7 _____

   _____

   3:8-15 _____

   _____

4:1-17 _____

_____

5:1-8 _____

_____

5:9-14 _____

_____

6:1-14 _____

_____

7:1-10 _____

_____

8:1-17 _____

_____

9:1-19 _____

_____

9:20-32 _____

_____

10:1-3 _____

_____

7. What other first impressions or observations
would you like to record and remember?

_____

_____

_____

_____

_____

8. From your answers to questions 2-7, what are
some of the themes of the book of Esther? (That

is, what is it about? What message does it have for Jews living under foreign occupation or for Christians in our day? Don't worry if you can't give a perfect answer; this is just your preliminary view.)

_____

_____

_____

_____

_____

_____

_____

_____

9. If your first reading of Esther has raised any questions about the book, write them down. Later lessons will probably answer some of them.

_____

_____

_____

_____

_____

10. To what areas of your life does the book of Esther currently seem relevant? Does your first look at it suggest any matters for prayer or action this week? Write down your thoughts and plans for application.

_____

_____

_____

_____

_____

_____

_____

_____

_____

For the group

If you are beginning with Esther and have not done
Ruth, you may get some good ideas from the "For
the group" sections in lessons one and two, pages
18-20 and 29-31.

Warm-up. Ask, "How does God act in your life?
What is the most recent thing you remember Him
saying to you or doing in your life?" This question
may not seem relevant at first, but it may be helpful
background when you discuss why neither God nor
any aspect of religion or faith is mentioned in the
book of Esther.

Read aloud and summarize. It would be a good idea
to read the whole book aloud during your meeting.
Jews enjoy doing this annually on Purim—they
assign the roles of narrator, Mordecai, Esther,
Xerxes, Vashti, Haman and the counselors to different people and encourage the actors to ham up their
roles. Booing and cheering are common. However, if
you can't spare the time to read the whole book
aloud, have someone in the group tell the story in
his or her own words. When the teller is finished,
other group members can add key details he or she
has omitted.

Questions. In order to let you discover the book of
Esther for yourselves, this overview has deliberately
not pointed out some of the key features of the
book. It will be up to you to decide what the book is
about, and why the author presents the story as he
does.

For instance, why is feasting mentioned so
often in the book? What point does all that feasting
make for you?

Why is fasting mentioned? What is the point of

the fasts? Why do you suppose prayer is never mentioned in connection with the fasts, even though fasting was invariably an accompaniment to prayer?

In fact, why are God's name and any religious acts never mentioned at all?

You may not be able to answer all these questions and explain all your observations satisfactorily now, but you will understand much more after studying the story in more detail. For now, just try for a tentative statement of what the book is about, what it is intended to teach us. Also, try to think of at least one concrete way a Christian can apply the lessons of the book of Esther.

Vengeance. Some group members may be shocked by the way the Jews slaughter seventy-five thousand of their enemies at the end of the story. It may be more appropriate to discuss this issue in lesson eight or nine, but you can address it now if you like. Do read the box "Vengeance in the Old Testament" on pages 94-96 and keep in mind the Study Skills on interpreting narratives (pages 33, 97, and 107). You may also want to prepare ahead of time by reading relevant New Testament passages, such as Luke 6:27-38 and Romans 12:14-13:10. Self-defense and vengeance are issues on which Christians continue to disagree and on which many excellent books have been written, so you may not resolve them among yourselves. Try to see the merits of all sides of the debate, and pray about your personal convictions.

Wrap-up. It's difficult to study the book of Esther chapter by chapter, as one would study a Gospel or one of Paul's letters. Esther is a story that makes its point only as a whole. Therefore, instead of dividing the book into sections, lessons seven through ten will each focus on a different character in the story. You'll look first at King Xerxes—not the most important character, but one who, as king and husband, offers you a model of leadership to think hard about. Next you'll compare Mordecai and Haman, then try to apply their examples to yourselves. Then you'll consider Esther and what her actions can teach you. Finally, you'll come back to the question of God's role in this book that never mentions Him, and God's role in your own lives. This last lesson will also help you compare Ruth and Esther—both the books and the women—for common themes. All four lessons will explain some of the historical and other references in the book to give you as clear a picture of life in Susa as possible.

Explain to the group what it should expect in the next four lessons.

Worship. Does this book that never speaks of God prompt you to any thanksgiving or praise?

1. Packer, Tenney, and White, *The World of the Old Testament,* page 195. See pages 183-195.
2. *The NIV Study Bible,* page 720.
3. Joyce Baldwin, *Esther: an Introduction and Commentary* (Downers Grove, Illinois: InterVarsity Press, 1984), page 19. (This book is referred to hereafter as Baldwin.) See also Herodotus, *The Histories,* translated by A. D. Godley, volume 3 (Cambridge, Massachusetts: Harvard University Press, 1922), book 9, chapters 108-113.
4. Baxter, *Explore the Book,* volume 2, pages 262-263. Baxter refers to Herodotus, book 7, chapters 27-39.
5. Baldwin, pages 48-49; *The NIV Study Bible,* page 718.
6. This study guide follows those scholars who consider the book of Esther to be historically accurate. Anyone interested in the specifics of this debate should consult the commentaries, such as those listed on pages 117-118.
7. Robert Gordis, *Religion, Wisdom and History in the Book of Esther—A New Solution to an Ancient Crux, Journal of Biblical Literature,* volume 100, number 3 (1981), pages 375-378. See also Baldwin, pages 35-36.
8. Martin Luther, *Table Talk,* 22; quoted in Baldwin, page 52.

ESTHER 1:1-10:3

Xerxes: King and Husband

Xerxes was lord of his empire; he had complete power of life and death over everyone. He was in control—right? As you study the king of Persia, ask God to help you compare yourself to him.

Xerxes (1:1). *Ahasuerus* in most versions. Recall from pages 64-65 what Herodotus had to say about this king.

India to Cush (1:1). In modern terms, that is from Pakistan (where the Indus River drains) to northern Sudan (ancient Ethiopia).[1] See the map on page 61.

Citadel of Susa (1:2). Xerxes' father Darius built Susa ("Shushan" in KJV) as his winter residence. The citadel ("capital" in RSV and NASB; "palace" in KJV) was on a hill west of the city; it was both an impregnable fortress 120 feet above the plain and a pleasure house for the court. A river watered the fabulous **garden** (1:5).[2]

Third year of his reign (1:3). That is, 483-482 BC (see the chronology on page 63). It took some time after his father's death for Xerxes to secure his throne against rivals and quell uprisings in Egypt and Babylon. Then he devoted himself to finishing the citadel of Susa that Darius had begun.[3] With these tasks accomplished, Xerxes was ready to apply himself to empire-building.

For Thought and Discussion: What do you think a godly woman should do if her husband gives a command like the one Xerxes gave Vashti (1:10-12)? Should her response be different if his demand is indecent? Should a woman accept orders from her husband at all? Base your answers on New Testament teaching.

He invited all the prominent men of his empire to spend six months in Susa, to admire his wealth and power and to help him plan a campaign against Greece. (From Herodotus we know that Xerxes fought a disastrous war with Greece in 482-479 BC.)[4]

Esther 1:3-5 probably doesn't mean that the banquet lasted *180 days* (1:4). Rather, the gathering of Persian leaders and the display of wealth lasted that long, but the banquet of 1:3 and 1:5 is the same—a seven-day debauch for all the workers and visitors in the citadel. This was the culmination and celebration of the half-year's planning for the attack on Greece.[5]

White and blue (1:6). White and blue-violet were the royal colors (see 8:15). The royal garden of Susa, which formerly had a pavilion for parties and a *mosaic pavement*, has been found by archaeologists.[6] In a few verses, the author paints for us a picture of luxury with hangings, gilt couches, and precious stones.

To drink in his own way (1:8). By Persian law, every guest had to drink every time the king drank.[7] Xerxes magnanimously waived this rule for those unable to keep up with him.

The author makes a point of the many times Xerxes drinks in this story (1:10, 3:15, 5:6, 7:2); indeed, the Hebrew word for "banquet" is related to the word for "to drink."[8]

Queen Vashti refused to come (1:12). No reason is given, as though no excuse would have been recognized as valid. Some have suggested that Xerxes asked her to come wearing *only* her crown (1:11).[9]

Wise men who understood the times (1:13). Royal advisors who could judge propitious times for action according to the stars and were also experts in politics and Persian law. These men "saw the king's face" (1:14, RSV); they talked with him face to face, a rare privilege.[10]

Cannot be repealed (1:19). Esther 8:8 and Daniel 6:8 also mention this fact, which is crucial to the story of Esther.

Later (2:1). Since Esther was crowned in the seventh year of Xerxes' reign (2:16), the king must have forgotten about finding a new queen during the war with Greece. After the embarassing Greek victory, Xerxes solaced himself with a new batch of girls for his harem.

Virgins for the king (2:2). The beauty contest described in 2:2-4,8-14 was no lucky chance for the girls. They were guaranteed a lifetime of frustrated isolation in the harem, unable to see their families. In exchange, they might spend only one night of their lives with their royal husband and never again see a man (other than the eunuch servants) or have children. Luxurious food and clothes they would have, but their quarters were hot and cramped. Back home in their villages, some of the young men would have to go without wives because the pretty girls were taken for the king.[11]

For Thought and Discussion: What do you think of the way laws were made in Persia (1:10-21, 3:8-15, 8:3-8)? What does God expect of lawmakers? Pray for your lawmakers.

For Further Study: How well did Xerxes live up to Proverbs 11:2, 17:1, 25:28?

1. The Jewish author probably wanted us to evaluate the characters in Esther with Old Testament teaching in mind. How well did Xerxes measure up to the standards in the following passages from Proverbs? (Write down what the proverbs teach and how Xerxes did or didn't conform to them.)

Teaching in Proverbs	How Xerxes measured up
Proverbs 5:15-19, 31:3	Esther 2:1-4,12-14

Teaching in Proverbs	How Xerxes measured up
Proverbs 31:4-9	Esther 1:10, 3:15, 5:6, 7:2
Proverbs 11:4	Esther 1:4
Proverbs 14:29	Esther 1:12,19-22; 7:7-10

Teaching in Proverbs	How Xerxes measured up
Proverbs 16:12-13; 20:26,28; 28:16; 29:12	Esther 3:8-11, 6:1-10, 7:3-10

2. What would you say were Xerxes' priorities? What did he value? (See, for instance, 1:4-15,22; 2:2; 6:1-3; 8:8.)

_____

_____

_____

_____

_____

_____

3. Consider how Xerxes dealt with women— Vashti, Esther, and the virgins of his kingdom. What good or bad examples did he set for men (especially husbands)? (See 1:10-12, 1:13-22, 2:1-4, 2:15-18, 5:1-8, 7:1-10, 8:1-8, 9:11-15.)

_____

_____

_____

_____

For Thought and Discussion: What should a Christian do if she finds herself married to or working for a man who shows traits like Xerxes'? Support your view from the New Testament. (Consider some of the following: Luke 6:27-42; Romans 12:17-21; 14:1-23; 2 Timothy 2:22-26; Hebrews 10:23-25; 13:4; James 3:13-18; 1 Peter 2:1,18-25; 3:1-22; 4:12-16; 5:6-11.)

Optional Application: Does some man in your life remind you of Xerxes? If so, pray for him, ask God to help you forgive and love him, and meditate this week on 1 Peter 2:13-3:6.

_____

_____

_____

_____

_____

_____

_____

4. Now evaluate Xerxes as a ruler.

   a. How did he go about making decisions (1:10-21; 2:1-17; 3:1,8-11; 5:1-8; 6:1-10; 7:1-10; 8:1-13; 9:11-14)?

_____

_____

_____

_____

_____

_____

_____

   b. How did Xerxes treat his subjects (1:4-8; 2:3,12-14; 3:11; 8:11; 10:1)?

_____

_____

_____

_____

_____

_____

5. Examine your own priorities, ways of dealing with people, and ways of making decisions in light of what Xerxes did. Are you like him in any good or bad ways? If so, how?

_____

_____

_____

_____

_____

_____

_____

6. Does a study of Xerxes make you want to change any of your habits, priorities, methods, or decisions? If so, what would you like to change (either to be more like Xerxes in some way, to be less like him, or to treat men like him differently)?

_____

_____

_____

_____

_____

7. What prayer and/or action can you pursue during the next week to begin changing in this area?

_____

_____

_____

_____

_____

For Thought and Discussion: Who or what controlled Xerxes' life? Explain your answer with specific passages. Then ask yourself who or what controls your life.

Optional Application: Meditate on one of the proverbs in question 1 and on how it applies to you. You might post it somewhere visible in your home or office.

8. Write down any questions you have about the material in this lesson.

_____

_____

_____

_____

For the group

Warm-up. Ask everyone to think of one person under his or her authority—employee, co-worker, wife, child—who has ever defied his or her will when given an instruction. Ask group members to remember what they did and how they felt when defied. This should help you each to identify with Xerxes.

Summarize. Instead of reading passages aloud, let a different group member tell what Xerxes does in 1:1-22; 2:1-4,17-18; 3:1,8-11,15; 5:1-8; 6:1-10; 7:1-10; 8:1-13; and 9:11-15. Members can read important sentences aloud to give the flavor of Xerxes' words and actions. This will help you remember the order of events and the details when you discuss question 1.

Questions. First state, then evaluate, Xerxes' behavior and priorities. Then discuss how you are tempted to be like him. Women's groups may be tempted to identify their bosses or husbands with Xerxes and so criticize them; if you are women, consider instead the ways in which you are like Xerxes (or would be if you had his power).

Also, consider how a Christian should deal with a man like Xerxes. In what ways do Vashti and Esther set good and bad examples for you? Support your views from the New Testament. What would you do if you were married to or working for a man like Xerxes? How does this help you to deal with your own situation?

If your group includes both men and women, direct some application questions toward men and some toward women. Each sex may learn from hearing the other's (especially spouses') view of how they are like Xerxes or should deal with men like Xerxes.

Some group members may feel they need more extended counseling or prayer to forgive and act in a godly manner. See that such needs are met, even if you don't have time for them during this group meeting. You can take a second meeting for more prayer and discussion, if necessary. Or, you can plan time alone with some members.

Summarize.

Worship. Thank God for revealing your faults to you and for providing you with the ability to change. Thank Him for enabling you to deal with men and women like Xerxes in godly ways.

1. Baldwin, page 56.
2. Joyce Baldwin, "Esther," *The New Bible Commentary: Revised,* edited by Donald Guthrie, et al. (Grand Rapids, Michigan: William B. Eerdmans Publishing Company, 1970), page 413. (Not cited hereafter.)
3. Herodotus, book 7, chapters 1-4; Baldwin, page 56.
4. Herodotus (book 7, chapters 8-20) tells how "After the conquest of Egypt . . . Xerxes held an assembly of the noblest among the Persians" (chapter 8) to decide whether and how to attack Greece.
5. Baldwin, page 57.
6. Baldwin, page 20.
7. Baldwin, pages 58-59.
8. Baldwin, page 56.
9. Baldwin, page 60.
10. *The NIV Study Bible,* page 720; Baldwin, page 61.
11. Baldwin, pages 67-68.

ESTHER 1:1-10:3

Mordecai and Haman

Mordecai and Haman agreed on a few things: both men knew they were not in total control of their own lives, that they each had a destiny to fulfill. However, one tiny disagreement about the nature of destiny raised Mordecai to the highest post in the empire and Haman to the highest gallows.

Ask God to speak to you through the examples of Mordecai and Haman. Then study the passages in the questions on pages 88-93, with the notes on pages 85-88 to help you understand the story.

Jew of the tribe of Benjamin (2:5). "Jew" technically meant a man from Judah, but after the
exile it was applied to Israelites of all tribes.
Jair, Shimei, and ***Kish*** were probably not Mordecai's immediate ancestors; Mordecai was too
young to be the great-grandson of the Kish who
was exiled in 597 BC. Rather, as was common in
ancient genealogies, 2:5 names three of Mordecai's prominent ancestors (1 Samuel 9:1,
2 Samuel 16:5). Those names show that Mordecai was of the family of King Saul. Since the
family went into exile with King ***Jehoiachin***
(the Hebrew *Jeconiah* is a variant of that name)
in 597 BC, it was probably one of the noble
houses of Judah (2 Kings 24:8-17, 25:27-30).[1]
   Mordecai (2:5) "incorporates Marduk, the
name of the state god of Babylon, and may be a
Hebrew version of the common [Babylonian and

85

Persian] name Mardukaya."[2] Like Joseph (Genesis 41:45), Daniel and his friends (Daniel 1:6-7), and Esther (Esther 2:7), Mordecai probably had two names, one among Jews and another among Gentiles.

Sitting at the king's gate (2:19). Recall from Ruth that the gate was the court for commercial and legal business (Ruth 4:1-11). The king's gate was the entrance to his palace, the citadel that towered above Susa. There the king's officials sat, and people seeking justice could come and stand before them. Upon becoming queen, Esther apparently had her cousin "appointed a magistrate or judge, 'a lesser position in the elaborate hierarchy of Persian officials.'"[3] Esther's loyalty coincidentally put Mordecai in position to overhear the other officials at the gate (Esther 2:21). She couldn't give Mordecai a higher position without disclosing her relationship to him (2:10,20).

There was room for ***all the royal officials at the king's gate*** (3:2). The gate at Persepolis, another Persian palace, has been excavated and measures more than sixty yards wide by thirty deep, with a wide stairway approaching it and "huge lion-like figures" flanking it.[4]

Gallows (2:23, 5:14, 7:9). The Persians normally executed people by impaling (hanging) them with nails on wooden poles in public view, as a lesson for the populace. The Hebrew word for "tree" was used for any tree, pole, or gallows (that is why Acts 5:30 and 1 Peter 2:24 speak of Jesus as hung on a "tree").[5]

Agagite (3:1). Haman was no more an ethnic Persian than Mordecai. He was descended from Agag, king of Amalek (1 Samuel 15:20). Israel was perpetually at war with Amalek because Amalek attacked Israel after the Exodus (Exodus 17:8-16, Deuteronomy 25:17-19). Israel was supposed to kill every Amalekite and destroy all captured property, taking no plunder (1 Samuel 15:1-3). However, King Saul gave in to his army's demand for plunder, and he also spared the life of King Agag. For these sins, Saul lost his kingship over Israel (1 Samuel 15:7-33). Yet five hundred years later, in the court of Xerxes, a descendant of Saul confronted a descendant of Agag, giving the family a second chance to obey the Lord.

For Thought and Discussion: Why did God want to reenact the battle between Israel and Amalek? What do you think this ancient feud was supposed to teach Israel? What should it teach us?

This ancestral feud was one reason why Haman was out to get the Jews and why Mordecai refused to honor Haman. Also, in Jewish eyes, the ancient command to kill all Amalekites justified the slaughter of Haman's family and allies. As instructed in 1 Samuel 15:3, the Jews took no plunder when they killed their enemies (Esther 9:10,15).

Knelt down (3:2). It was customary to bow like this before one's superiors, so Joyce Baldwin suspects there was "a general lack of respect for this man [Haman], otherwise there should have been no need for a royal command. . . ."[6] It was not against the Israelite faith to bow down before people (Genesis 23:7, 33:3, 44:14; 1 Samuel 20:41, 24:8; 2 Samuel 14:4; 1 Kings 1:16). Mordecai probably refused to honor Haman either because he was personally offensive or because he was an Amalekite.

The pur (3:7). Many peoples in the ancient Near East cast lots to receive guidance. People thought that fate was predetermined, and that humans could succeed only if they cooperated with destiny. Signs and omens in the stars, nature, and elsewhere revealed fate to the knowledgeable, and everything was scheduled according to lucky days.

An Assyrian "cube-shaped dice" has been discovered that dates from around 858-824 BC, inscribed with a sentence that twice uses the word *puru*. In Assyria lots or dice were cast each year to chose the "'eponym official,' whose name was used in chronological tables to signify a certain year of a king's reign."[7] The Assyrians also used dice each New Year's Day to choose dates for important occasions of the coming year. Apparently, courtiers in Persia were still setting their calendars for the year by the same method 350 years later.

Ten thousand talents (3:9). Herodotus "records that the annual income of the Persian empire was 15,000 talents. If this figure is correct, Haman offers two-thirds of that amount—a huge sum. Presumably the money would have come from the plundered wealth of the victims of the decree."[8]

Xerxes seems to turn down the money in 3:11, and 3:13 suggests that the Jews' attackers would be allowed to plunder them. However, 4:7 and 7:4 suggest that the king would receive at least some of the proceeds.

Signet ring (3:10,12). A document was made official by stamping the king's ring in wax on it. The wax seal served as the king's signature.[9]

Tore his clothes . . . sackcloth and ashes . . . wailing (4:1). These were normal signs of grief in the ancient world, where people expressed their emotions much more than modern westerners do. **Mourning** and **fasting** (4:3) in such situations were almost certainly the physical acts that went with prayer, but the author deliberately did not mention any plea to God for help.[10]

One of the king's eunuchs (4:5). Mordecai and Esther had to speak through a eunuch messenger because the queen was isolated from men in the harem and because Mordecai could not enter the citadel in mourning clothes.

1. On one level, the book of Esther reveals a clash between men of contrasting personalities and ethics. What do you learn about Haman from the following passages? (Observe as many details as possible.)

   3:1-15 _____

   _____

   _____

   _____

   _____

   _____

   _____

5:9-14 _____

_____

_____

_____

_____

_____

6:4-14 _____

_____

_____

_____

_____

_____

7:6-8 _____

_____

_____

_____

2. How does Haman's life exemplify Proverbs
   3:33-35; 6:16-19; 11:2; 14:22; 16:5,18?

_____

_____

_____

_____

_____

_____

_____

_____

Optional Application: a. What were the results of pride and hatred in Haman's life?

b. Do you regard your status at all as Haman did? Do you feel about anyone as he felt about Mordecai? How can you avoid Haman's sins?

Optional Application: Do any of the proverbs in question 2 suggest an area of your life you need to pray about and act on? If so, what will you do?

For Thought and Discussion: What would you have done in Mordecai's place in 2:21-22, 3:2-4, 5:9? Why?

For Further Study: Compare Mordecai to Boaz. What traits do they have in common, and how do they differ?

3. Describe Mordecai's personality and ethics from his behavior in these passages.

2:19-23 _____

_____

_____

_____

_____

_____

3:1-4 _____

_____

_____

_____

4:1-17 _____

_____

_____

_____

_____

_____

_____

_____

_____

_____

5:9 _____

_____

_____

_____

8:1-2,9-10,15 _____

_____

_____

_____

_____

9:20 _____

_____

_____

_____

9:4, 10:3 _____

_____

_____

_____

_____

Optional Application: Mordecai was the person who moved Esther to act on behalf of the Jews. Why did she obey him (2:10,20; 4:12-16)? How can you influence others as Mordecai did?

Optional Application: What opportunity do you have to imitate Mordecai in 2:21-22? Pray about this carefully.

4. On a deeper level, the story depicts a conflict between two views of how the world works.

   a. In Haman's view, what controlled the events of history and individual lives (3:7)?

   _____

   _____

   _____

   b. How did this belief affect the way Haman conducted his life?

   _____

   _____

   _____

   _____

   _____

5. a. According to Mordecai, what controlled history and human destiny (4:12-14)?

_____

_____

_____

_____

_____

_____

_____

_____

b. When Mordecai saw the Controller of History at work, did he sit passively by and let events take their course? What did he do, and why (4:1,8,12-17)?

_____

_____

_____

_____

_____

_____

_____

_____

6. What lessons for our lives does the clash between Mordecai and Haman teach?

_____

_____

_____

_____

_____

_____

_____

_____

_____

7. Which of these lessons would you like to apply to your own life?

_____

_____

_____

_____

_____

8. How can you pray, choose, and/or act this week in light of this lesson?

_____

_____

_____

_____

_____

_____

9. Write down any questions you have about this study or the book of Esther.

_____

_____

_____

_____

_____

For the group

Warm-up. Ask, "Do you think you have a destiny? If so, who or what set that destiny, and who or what will bring it to pass? If not, why not?" Don't get into a long, speculative discussion of destiny; just let the group think about it briefly, perhaps letting each person give a short statement of his or her view. By the end of your discussion, you should have a clearer view of what the book of Esther says about destiny.

Read aloud. To set the scene, have someone read 3:1-11 and another read 4:1-17.

Summarize. What is the focus of this lesson?

Questions. Try to see how your actions and assumptions resemble Haman's, and how you can act according to Mordecai's character traits and beliefs. Encourage each group member to find one specific area of his or her life in which to become more like Mordecai and less like Haman, or one specific action he or she can take in light of what these men show about life.

Vengeance. If you plan to discuss the box "Vengeance in the Old Testament," see the relevant paragraph in the "For the group" on page 72 and also the Study Skills on pages 33, 97, and 107.

Summarize.

Worship. Praise God for being in control of history in an active, personal, loving way. Thank Him for showing you that chance and impersonal fate do not control your lives. Thank Him also for giving you responsibility, and ask Him to make you more like Mordecai and less like Haman.

Vengeance in the Old Testament

Christians have often been uncomfortable with the book of Esther because it celebrates an event when the Jews were enabled "to avenge themselves on their enemies" (8:13) by killing "seventy-five thousand of them" (9:16). Vengeance is considered unChristian, for we must

(continued on page 95)

(continued from page 94)

"not repay anyone evil for evil" but instead "overcome evil with good" (Romans 12:17,20). We must love our enemies, turn the other cheek, and let the thief take our tunic along with our cloak (Luke 6:27-31). Does Esther reflect an Old Testament Jewish vindictiveness that nonviolent Christians must reject?

First, consider the word *vengeance* itself. It comes from the Latin *vindicare* which also gives us *vindicate* and *vindictive*. To vindicate oneself is to attain justice; no one would call that undesirable. But to be vindictive is to desire justice with hatred and condemnation. Christians reject that spirit (Luke 6:37-38; Romans 12:19-20; Ephesians 4:26,32). Also, should a Christian even forgo earthly vindication if attaining justice requires violence?

The Hebrew word in Esther 8:13 can mean both vengeance and vindication. In the former sense, the Old Testament forbids individuals to take vengeance or harbor vengeful feelings (Genesis 4:15, Leviticus 19:18, Deuteronomy 32:35-36, Proverbs 25:21-22), although Israelites often did take personal revenge against God's will (Genesis 34). God insisted that He alone had the right to avenge wrongs, and He promised to avenge Himself impartially against Israel as well as its enemies (Leviticus 26:25; Isaiah 1:24-25; Jeremiah 5:9,29).

The author of Esther assumes we know that personal vengeance and vindictive feelings are forbidden. He stresses that the Jews killed only those who attacked them on one (two in Susa) prescribed day, and that they did not profit materially from the deaths (Esther 9:1-2,5,10,16). "They did what they pleased to those who hated them" (Esther 9:5) does not suggest an orgy of cruelty, but only a free hand from the Persian authorities to defend themselves. The Jews acted to defend their nation against extinction; this was no private vendetta. The author implies that the edict allowing the Jews to fight was semi-miraculous, possible only by God's intervention, and so was in effect His act of vengeance.[11]

Where does this leave us as Christians? Both
(continued on page 96)

(continued from page 95)

Old and New Testaments condemn private vengeance and vindictive desires, but the Old Testament seems to condone national defense. Jesus, Paul, and the rest spoke to private persons, not nations, so Christians continue to disagree over whether nations and groups may use violence to defend themselves. From your reading of Scripture, what do you think?

1. Baldwin, page 65; *The NIV Study Bible,* page 721.
2. Baldwin, page 65.
3. Baldwin, page 70; quoting Robert Gordis, "Studies in the Esther Narrative," *Journal of Biblical Literature,* volume 95, number 1 (1976), page 48.
4. Baldwin, page 72.
5. *The NIV Study Bible,* page 722.
6. Baldwin, page 72.
7. Baldwin, pages 22-23, quoting W. W. Hallo, "The First Purim," *The Biblical Archaeologist,* volume 46, number 1 (1983), page 22.
8. *The NIV Study Bible,* page 723; referring to Herodotus, book 3, chapter 95.
9. D. Miall Edwards, "Seal," *The International Standard Bible Encyclopaedia,* volume 4 (Grand Rapids, Michigan: William B. Eerdmans Publishing Company, 1956), pages 2708-2709.
10. Baldwin, pages 76-77.
11. Baldwin, pages 100-102.

ESTHER 1:1-10:3

Esther

In a way, Esther was Ruth's opposite: a Jewess who married a ruthless pagan despot, not a Moabitess who married a devout Jewish farmer. But in other ways, the two women were in similar positions. As you study Esther, think about Ruth and yourself.

Study Skill—Interpreting and Applying Old Testament Narratives

You read some of Fee and Stuart's principles on pages 33-34; here are some more:

7. "Narratives record what happened—not necessarily what should have happened or what ought to happen every time. Therefore not every narrative [or every piece of a narrative] has an individual identifiable moral of the story."

8. "What people do in narratives is not necessarily a good example for us. Frequently, it is just the opposite."

9. "Most of the characters in Old Testament narratives are far from perfect and their actions are, too."

10. "We are not always told at the end of a narrative whether what happened was good or bad. We are expected to be able to judge that on the basis of what God has taught us directly and categorically already in the Scripture."[1]

Keep these guidelines in mind when you think about issues like vengeance (see pages 94-96).

Hadassah . . . Esther (2:7). The Hebrew name Hadassah means "myrtle," a plant that for the Jews symbolized peace with God and prosperity (Isaiah 41:19, 55:13). The Persian name Esther means "star"; it sounds like Hadassah and suggests the star-shaped myrtle flowers, but it is related to the name of the Babylonian goddess Ishtar.[2]

Taken (2:8). The girls were probably not forced, but to refuse the summons would have meant instant death.

Favor (2:9,17). *Hesed* (see the note on Ruth 1:8 on page 25). In the Old Testament, *hesed* is normally used for God's covenant love—His lovingkindness or steadfast love to His covenant people. Seeing this word twice in one chapter of Esther would have reminded Jewish readers of the divine *hesed* toward Esther and her people. (Recall from Ruth 1:8, 2:20, 3:10 that Ruth and Boaz showed *hesed* toward their kin in the sense of kindness or covenant loyalty, but Hegai's and Xerxes' *hesed* was kindness or favor that came from someone else's covenant loyalty.)

Another word for "favor" occurs in Esther 2:15; 5:2,8; 7:3; 8:5 to emphasize the theme of favor in the book.

Without being summoned (4:11). It's not clear why Esther didn't just request an audience with the king instead of going to the throne room unannounced. Perhaps she expected a long delay before she could get an appointment, especially because her fickle husband hadn't even asked to see her for a month. Isolated as she was in the harem, she had few ways of knowing what political concerns were occupying him, what mood he was in, or whether another of his women was his current favorite.

Banquet (5:4). The king and queen were not alone in the throne room; there were inevitably retainers, guards, Persian officials, and even perhaps foreigners present on state business. Esther wisely planned to make her request in a more private, less formal setting, where the king would not be seen publicly to change his mind about a law because of his wife's influence.[3]

1. What do you learn about Esther from
   2:7,9,10,15,17,20?

   _____

   _____

   _____

   _____

   _____

   _____

   _____

   _____

For Further Study:
How did Esther exem-
plify or not exemplify
Proverbs 11:22;
13:1,3; 24:11-12?
How can you practice
or avoid these
qualities?

2. Why was she reluctant to approach her husband
   to save her people and herself (4:10-11)?

   _____

   _____

   _____

   _____

   _____

3. Consider her final decision and her words to
   Mordecai. What does 4:12-16 tell you about
   Esther's character, priorities, and beliefs?

   _____

   _____

   _____

   _____

   _____

   _____

   _____

For Further Study:
For some reasons why
Old Testament people
fast, look up
1 Samuel 7:6,
2 Samuel 12:15-16,
Ezra 8:21, Nehemiah
9:1-3, Joel 2:12-17.

**For Thought and
Discussion:** Put
yourself in Esther's
place. Your fickle
husband hasn't called
you for a month, and
to approach him
unwanted means
death. On the other
hand, if you don't
appeal to him, then
you and your people
will be killed. What
will you do, and why?

4. Why do you think Esther wanted all the Jews in
Susa to fast for three days with her (4:16)?
(What does this reveal about her and her
beliefs? What did fasting signify?)

_____

_____

_____

_____

_____

5. Should Christians fast? If so, for what purposes?
If not, why not? (*Optional:* See Isaiah 58:1-14;
Matthew 6:16-18, 9:14-17; James 4:7-10.)

_____

_____

_____

_____

_____

_____

6. Esther probably asked Xerxes and Haman to the
first banquet to avoid making her request public
(5:4). Her reason for postponing the request
again (5:7-8) is less obvious.

a. What did this second delay accomplish
(5:9-6:14)?

_____

_____

_____

_____

_____

b. Could Esther have foreseen these events? Why do you think she decided to wait another day? (*Optional:* Compare Esther 4:16 to Proverbs 3:5-6, 16:3.)

_____

_____

_____

_____

_____

7. What examples does Esther set that we should follow?

_____

_____

_____

_____

_____

8. Esther hid her Jewishness for five years (Esther 2:10,20). During that time, unlike Daniel (Daniel 1:8-16), she did not avoid food offered to idols or other nonkosher food (Esther 2:9, 5:4-6), nor did she openly worship the God of Israel. As queen, she must have had to attend events in honor of the Persian gods. Was she right or wrong to do this? Why?

_____

_____

_____

_____

_____

Optional Application: Do you have influence with anyone—a husband, boss, etc.—as Esther did? How can you use your influence to serve God and help people, without being sneaky or manipulative? What might it cost you to do this?

For Thought and Discussion: Which of Esther's actions are not good examples for us, and why?

For Thought and Discussion: Compare Esther to Ruth. How are they alike and different?

For Thought and Discussion: Under what circumstances is it right, and under what circumstances is it not right, for a Christian to hide his or her faith in Christ? Can we follow Esther's example in this area? What does the New Testament say about this?

9. a. Mordecai saved his pagan king's life but refused to bow to Haman, his official superior (2:21-22, 3:2). Esther broke the law by approaching the king without an appointment (4:11, 5:1). What moved Esther and Mordecai to disobey the law in each case?

_____

_____

_____

_____

_____

_____

_____

b. Why do you think they were generally obedient to the law and loyal to the king, even though Xerxes was a tyrant and the Persians were pagans?

_____

_____

_____

_____

_____

_____

_____

c. Are there any lessons here for Christians living under nonChristian governments?

_____

_____

_____

_____

102

For Further Study:
Study what the apostles Paul and Peter said to Christians under nonChristian regimes (Romans 13:1-7,11-14; 1 Peter 2:13-17). Did Esther and Mordecai live up to this New Testament standard? How is it relevant to your life?

_____

_____

_____

_____

10. In what one way would you like to apply Esther's example to your own attitudes and actions?

_____

_____

_____

_____

_____

_____

11. How can you practice this or begin to make it more of a habit? Describe your plans for prayer and action during the next week or so.

_____

_____

_____

_____

_____

_____

12. List any questions you have about this lesson.

_____

_____

_____

_____

_____

For the group

Warm-up. Ask everyone to think of one time in his or her life when it was risky or uncomfortable to be known as a Christian. Why was it risky or uncomfortable? A question like this helps people identify with Esther and, if you share your experiences, helps you to get to know each other better.

Summarize. What is this lesson about?

Questions. Use question 1 as background to refresh everyone's memory about Esther. Let different people tell what she does in each scene and what they learn about her from her words and actions. Then discuss how Esther's example applies to you (question 7).

Next, focus on the central episodes: 4:4-5:8 (questions 2-6). Observe what Esther does, interpret why she does it, and evaluate whether or not it is a good example for Christians. Discuss specific ways you can apply the good examples.

Questions 8 and 9 raise some moral issues that we face as Esther did. Evaluate her decisions regarding concealing her faith and disobeying authority. Was she right or wrong in each case? What should a Christian do in a similar situation? Are you in any similar situations?

Finally, give each person a chance to share his or her plans for personal application. Does anyone want prayer? Does anyone prefer to keep working on an application from lesson eight? Is anyone having difficulty with application?

Summarize.

Worship. Thank God for what you are learning through the book of Esther. Ask Him to help you respond to crises as Esther did.

Lots and Portions

A portion in Hebrew culture was in one sense a gift signifying favor. Joseph gave his brothers portions, and his favorite brother received the largest portion (Genesis 43:34). Nebuchadnezzar honored Daniel and others by giving them special portions of food (Daniel 1:5), and Evil-

(continued on page 105)

(continued from page 104)
Merodach allotted Jehoiachin a portion at the king's table for life (2 Kings 25:27-30). In Esther, portions signified Hegai's favor for Esther (Esther 2:9) and the Jews' love for each other in the Purim celebration (Esther 9:19,22; compare Nehemiah 8:10).

A portion was also one's lot in life: different portions of sacrificial animals were allotted to the various groups in the Temple (Nehemiah 12:44,47; 13:10); a righteous man's portion is the Lord and blessings from Him (Psalm 16:5-6); but a wicked man's is destruction (Jeremiah 13:24-25).

Thus, one's portion was the destiny appointed not by blind fate, but by the Sovereign Lord, who gave love-gifts to those whom He favored. God overturned the Jews' portion decreed by Haman's lots (Esther 3:7). The portions shared at Purim (9:19,22) celebrated that a person's lot or portion was a gift from God.

The Hebrew word-plays on lots and portions in Esther don't translate well into English, but punning was a favorite way in which the Old Testament writers made their points.[4]

---

1. Fee and Stuart, page 78.
2. Baldwin, pages 65-66.
3. Baldwin, page 86.
4. Baldwin, pages 112-114.

REVIEW OF ESTHER

The Lord of History

We've scarcely mentioned God since we began studying Esther because, as you've probably noticed, the book itself never mentions Him. Where was God while His chosen people were threatened with annihilation? Where is He in your life?

Study Skill—Interpretation Errors to Avoid

Instead of reading a passage for what God wants to say through it, people sometimes try to find in it a message for their current lives that isn't really there. God's counsel for their present concerns may be somewhere else in the Bible, but people are impatient. Some errors such people fall into are:

1. *Allegorizing.* This involves making every person and thing in a passage a type or symbol of something else. For example, the Persian Jews represent worldy people, Mordecai represents the faithful Jewish remnant, Esther represents the Church, and so on. As we said on pages 53-54, when typology degenerates into allegorizing a book that is not allegory, it threatens to obscure the plain meaning of the text. It isn't necessarily wrong to see types in Esther, but we should take the book literally first.

2. *Decontextualizing.* This means "ignoring the full historical and literary contexts" and instead concentrating on individual

(continued on page 108)

(continued from page 107)

verses or paragraphs from a modern point of view. For instance, one could take the word "avenge" in 8:13 out of the context of the rest of the story and the Old Testament.

3. *Selectivity.* This is building an interpretation on certain words and phrases, while ignoring other phrases and "the overall sweep of the passage." For example, one could use Esther as an example of how a woman should be outwardly submissive to men in authority (2:10,20; 4:11), but should privately manipulate men to do what she wants (5:1-4, 7:1-6, 8:1-6).

4. *False Combination.* This entails combining unconnected elements in a passage and drawing a conclusion from the combination. For instance, Esther hid her identity and Haman plotted to kill the Jews; therefore, the whole plot was ultimately Esther's fault, the result of concealing her faith.

5. *Redefinition.* When the plain meaning of the text says something people don't want to hear or aren't interested in, they may redefine it to mean something else. For example, since God is never mentioned in the book of Esther, it's clear that He did not approve of the Jews killing for self-defense.

1. Skim through the book of Esther and note the verse reference and a brief description of at least six coincidences or "lucky" occurrences in the story.

(2:9) Hegai liked Esther best; she won his favor (hesed)

_____

_____

_____

_____

_____

_____

For Thought and Discussion: How was God's role in the Persian crisis similar to His activity in Ruth's and Naomi's lives? Is His presence in your life similar?

2. Even though neither God nor prayer nor worship is ever mentioned in the book, was God absent from the events? What role do you think He played?

_____

_____

_____

_____

_____

_____

3. a. What principle does Proverbs 21:1 state?

_____

_____

_____

   b. How does the book of Esther illustrate this proverb (1:19-21, 2:17, 5:2, 6:1-10, 7:1-10, 8:1-8, 9:4)?

_____

_____

_____

_____

_____

_____

For Thought and Discussion: The Jews have survived another 2400 years since Mordecai's time, despite numerous attempts to annihilate them. Is God still protecting them? Support your view from such scriptures as Romans 9-11.

c. Is this proverb applicable to your life in any way? If so, how?

_____

_____

_____

_____

_____

4. Why was Mordecai certain that "deliverance for the Jews will arise" (Esther 4:14) from somewhere (Genesis 12:1-3, Isaiah 41:8-16)?

_____

_____

_____

_____

_____

_____

Mordecai knew this didn't mean God would never allow the Jews to be defeated. Israel had fallen to Assyria and Judah to Babylon; Jerusalem was still a shambles and the Jews still lived under foreign rule. Many Jews had died in those catastrophes, and Mordecai and Esther knew that it was possible that they might die in this one (Esther 4:14,16).

5. Why did God permit defeats but not total destruction (Deuteronomy 4:25-32, Isaiah 54:4-10)?

_____

_____

_____

_____

_____

_____

6. Can Christians count on God's favor just as Mordecai did? Why or why not (Romans 4:13-25, Ephesians 2:11-22)?

_____

_____

_____

_____

_____

_____

_____

_____

7. Does this mean that every individual Christian and group of Christians can expect God to protect them from violent death? If so, why? If not, how should we deal with threats to our survival? (See Esther 4:16. *Optional:* See Luke 12:4-12, 21:10-28; Acts 4:23-31, 5:41-42; Philippians 1:12-30.)

_____

_____

_____

_____

_____

_____

_____

_____

_____

_____

For Thought and Discussion: a. Were the Jews justified in killing thousands of their enemies (9:16)? Why or why not?

b. Would Christians be justified in doing the same thing in similar circumstances? Why or why not? Support your answer from Scripture.

111

Optional Application: What has God promised to accomplish in your life? What is your responsibility? Consider such promises as Luke 21:10-19, John 15:1-17, Acts 1:8.

8. a. Think about the stories of both Ruth and Esther. In these books, what responsibility do human beings (such as Ruth, Naomi, Boaz, Esther, and Mordecai) have in the fulfillment of God's plans?

_____

_____

_____

_____

_____

_____

   b. What kinds of things does God do to make sure that His plans work out?

_____

_____

_____

_____

_____

_____

9. What have you learned from this lesson that is relevant to your life? Write down as many implications as you can.

_____

_____

_____

_____

_____

_____

_____

_____

10. a. What one of these insights would you like to concentrate on for application this week?

_____

_____

_____

_____

_____

_____

b. How can you practice it through prayer and or action?

_____

_____

_____

_____

_____

_____

11. Look back at your answer to question 8 of lesson six (page 70). What do you now think the book of Esther is about? What are its main themes and lessons?

_____

_____

_____

_____

_____

_____

For Thought and Discussion: a. How have you been able to follow the examples of Ruth and Esther, Boaz and Mordecai?
b. What have you found difficult about applying the lessons of Ruth and Esther? What different tactics can you take?

12. Look back at the questions in lesson six through nine in which you described some application you wanted to make.

   a. Have you noticed any areas (thoughts, attitudes, opinions, behavior) in which you have changed as a result of studying Esther? If so, how have you changed?

   _____

   _____

   _____

   _____

   _____

   b. Ask God to show you any areas on which you should continue to concentrate for growth. Write any thoughts or plans here.

   _____

   _____

   _____

   _____

   _____

13. Review the questions you listed at the ends of lessons six through nine. Do any important ones remain unanswered? If so, some of the sources on pages 117-119 may help you find answers, or you can ask someone for help. Write your questions here.

   _____

   _____

   _____

   _____

   _____

   _____

For the group

Warm-up. Ask, "Do you feel in any way responsible for God's will getting done in your generation? Why or why not?"

Read aloud. Instead of reading large sections of the book, begin with question 1. Ask what coincidences group members found in chapter 1, then chapter 2, and so on. When you've finished, you'll have reminded everyone of the story's key events.

Summarize. Ask someone (or several people) what he or she thinks the main focus of this lesson is.

Questions. Questions 2-3 are straightforward, but questions 4-5 require some thinking. What promises of God did Mordecai count on? Can we count on those same promises? If so, what should be our attitude in doing so? Should we always, sometimes, or never sit passively and expect God to protect us? Why? Should we take action? If so, what kind? Is violent action ever acceptable? Think of some specific situations Christians might find themselves in (such as an anti-Christian totalitarian country, a hostile work situation, or a violent family).

Question 8 addresses a topic you discussed in lesson four, question 8. Does the book of Esther confirm or change your view of human and divine responsibility? How have you been able to apply this insight, and how can you do so in the future?

You've noticed that it takes some discernment and knowledge of the New Testament to decide which aspects of Esther apply to us and which were unique to the situation. Some difficult areas are violence for defense, hiding one's faith when marrying an unbeliever, and expecting God to defend Christian groups and individuals. Try summarizing a list of what lessons we *can* and *shouldn't* draw from Esther. What are the most important lessons for your lives?

Wrap-up. There are some things worth doing at the end of every study of a book to give the group a sense of completeness. First, give everyone a chance to ask questions about the book that haven't been answered. See if the group can answer them, or plan how you can find answers. Second, evaluate what you've learned, how well the group has liked your meetings, and what you will do next. Questions 12 and 13 are part of such an evaluation, but you might take part or all of another meeting to discuss the following questions:

> How well did the study help you to grasp the book of Esther?
> What were the most important truths you discovered together about the Lord?
> What did you like best about your meetings?
> What did you like least? What would you change?
> How well did you meet the goals you set at your first meeting?
> What did you learn about small group study?
> What are members' current needs and interests?
> What will you do next?

Worship. Praise God for being in control of history and for guarding His people. Thank Him for the responsibilities He has given each of you. Thank Him for what you've learned and how you've changed from studying Esther, and for the opportunity to study the Bible together. If your nation is safer than Persia, thank Him for that.

STUDY AIDS

For more information on Ruth and Esther, consider the following sources. If your local bookstore does not have them, you can have the bookstore order them from the publisher, or you can find them in most seminary libraries. Many university and public libraries also carry these books.

Commentaries on Ruth and Esther

Campbell, Edward F. *Ruth* (Anchor Bible, Doubleday, 1975).
> This work is much more thorough than Morris's, since it includes Campbell's own translation, lots of references to other scholarly works, cultural background, the flavor of Hebrew words, and detailed comments. For someone serious about delving into Ruth, this is an excellent work and not too technical.

Morris, Leon. *Ruth: an Introduction and Commentary* (Tyndale Old Testament Commentary Series, InterVarsity, 1968).
> Although less exhaustive than Campbell's book, this one gives about all of the commentary and background that the average student could want.

Baldwin, Joyce G. *Esther: an Introduction and Commentary* (Tyndale Old Testament Commentaries, InterVarsity, 1984).
> A fine study. Baldwin makes the available historical information on the Persian period easily accessible to the layman and brings the book of Esther alive. She deals quickly with the major higher critical issues in a way the average student can understand, but she focuses on interpreting the text.

Moore, Carey A. *Esther* (Anchor Bible, Doubleday, 1971).
> Less delightful to read than Baldwin, but full of fine comments on the meanings of phrases, the flavor of words, archaeological illustrations, and close analysis of the text.

Paton, Lewis B. *A Critical and Exegetical Commentary on the Book of Esther* (International Critical Commentary Series, Charles Scribner's Sons, 1908).

Paton gives much good historical and technical information for the serious student, although he feels that Esther includes fictional elements. The main commentary is very insightful, but the average student may prefer to skip Paton's analyses of textual variations and other scholarly issues.

Old Testament History and Culture

A **history** or **survey** traces Israel's history from beginning to end, so that you can see where each biblical event fits. *A Survey of Israel's History* by Leon Wood (Zondervan, 1970) is a good basic introduction for laymen from a conservative viewpoint. Not critical or heavily learned, but not simplistic. Many other good surveys are also available. On the Persian period, serious students will enjoy *History of the Persian Empire* by A. T. Olmstead (University of Chicago, 1948). Also, Herodotus's *Histories* are available in English translation from several publishers.

A ***Bible dictionary*** or ***Bible encyclopedia*** alphabetically lists articles about people, places, doctrines, important words, customs, and geography of the Bible.

The New Bible Dictionary, edited by J.D. Douglas, F.F. Bruce, J.I. Packer, N. Hillyer, D. Gutherie, A.R. Millard, and D.J. Wiseman (Tyndale, 1982) is more comprehensive than most dictionaries. Its 1300 pages include quantities of information along with excellent maps, charts, diagrams, and an index for cross-referencing.

Unger's Bible Dictionary by Merrill F. Unger (Moody, 1979) is equally excellent and is available in an inexpensive paperback edition.

The Zondervan Pictorial Encyclopedia edited by Merrill C. Tenney (Zondervan, 1975, 1976) is excellent and exhaustive. It is being revised and updated in the 1980s. However, its five 1000-page volumes are a financial investment, so all but very serious students may prefer to use it at a library.

A good ***Bible atlas*** can be a great aid to understanding what is going on in a book of the Bible and how geography affected events. Here are a few good choices:

The Macmillan Atlas by Yohanan Aharoni and Michael Avi-Yonah (Macmillan, 1968, 1977) contains 264 maps, 89 photos, and 12 graphics. The many maps of individual events portray battles, movements of people, and changing boundaries in detail.

The New Bible Atlas by J.J. Bimson and J.P. Kane (Tyndale, 1985) has 73 maps, 34 photos, and 34 graphics. Its evangelical perspective, concise and helpful text, and excellent research make it a good choice, but its greatest strength is its outstanding graphics, such as cross-sections of the Dead Sea.

The Bible Mapbook by Simon Jenkins (Lion, 1984) is much shorter and less expensive than most other atlases, so it offers a good first taste of the usefulness of maps. It contains 91 simple maps, very little text, and 20 graphics. Some of the graphics are computer-generated and intriguing.

The Moody Atlas of Bible Lands by Barry J. Beitzel (Moody, 1984) is scholarly, very evangelical, and full of theological text, indexes, and references. This admirable reference work will be too deep and costly for some, but Beitzel shows vividly how God prepared the land of Israel perfectly for the acts of salvation He was going to accomplish in it.

Yohanan Aharoni has also written *The Land of the Bible: A Historical Geography* (Westminster Press, 1967). After describing the mountains, deserts, winds, rains, and trade routes of ancient Palestine, Aharoni traces the Old Testament history of the promised land with maps and text. For instance, he shows how Abraham lived in Beersheba and how different Judah was from Galilee.

Old Testament Words

A *concordance* lists words of the Bible alphabetically along with each verse in which the word appears. It lets you do your own word studies. An *exhaustive* concordance lists every instance of every word in a given translation. An *abridged* or *complete* concordance omits either some words, some occurrences of the word, or both.

The two best exhaustive concordances are *Strong's Exhaustive Concordance* and *Young's Analytical Concordance to the Bible.* Both are based on the King James Version of the Bible. *Strong's* has an index by which you can find out which Greek or Hebrew word is used in a given English verse. *Young's* breaks up each English-word listing according to the Greek or Hebrew words it translates. Thus, you can cross-reference the original language's words without knowing that language.

Among other good, less expensive concordances, *Cruden's Complete Concordance* is keyed to the King James and Revised Versions, and *The NIV Complete Concordance* is keyed to the New International Version. These include all references to every word included, but they omit "minor" words. They also lack indexes to the original languages.

The Expository Dictionary of the Old Testament, edited by Merrill F. Unger and William White (Thomas Nelson, 1980) defines major biblical Hebrew words. It is not exhaustive, but it is adequate for the average Bible student who does not know Hebrew.

For Small Group Leaders

The Small Group Leader's Handbook by Steve Barker et al. (InterVarsity, 1982). Written by an InterVarsity small group with college students primarily in mind. It includes information on group dynamics and how to lead in light of them, and many ideas for worship, building community, and outreach. It has a good chapter on doing inductive Bible study.

Getting Together: A Guide for Good Groups by Em Griffin (InterVarsity, 1982). Applies to all kinds of groups, not just Bible studies. From his own experience, Griffin draws deep insights into why people join groups; how people relate to each other; and principles of leadership, decision-making, and discussions. It is fun to read, but its 229 pages will take more time than the above book.

You Can Start a Bible Study Group by Gladys Hunt (Harold Shaw, 1984). Builds on Hunt's thirty years of experience leading groups. This book is wonderfully focused on God's enabling. It is both clear and applicable for Bible study groups of all kinds.

How to Lead Small Groups by Neal F. McBride (NavPress, 1990). Covers leadership skills for all kinds of small groups—Bible study, fellowship, task, and support groups. Filled with step-by-step guidance and practical exercises to help you grasp the critical aspects of small group leadership and dynamics.

The Small Group Letter, a special section in Discipleship Journal (NavPress). Unique. Its four pages per issue, six issues per year are packed with practical ideas for small groups. It stays up to date because writers discuss what they are currently doing as small group members and leaders. To subscribe, write to Subscription Services, Post Office Box 54470, Boulder, Colorado 80323-4470.

Bible Study Methods

Braga, James. *How to Study the Bible* (Multnomah, 1982). Clear chapters on a variety of approaches to Bible study: synthetic, geographical, cultural, historical, doctrinal, practical, and so on. Designed to help the ordinary person without seminary training to use these approaches.

Fee, Gordon, and Douglas Stuart. *How to Read the Bible For All Its Worth* (Zondervan, 1982). After explaining in general what interpretation (exegesis) and application (hermeneutics) are, Fee and Stuart offer chapters on inter- preting and applying the different kinds of writing in the Bible: Epistles, Gospels, Old Testament Law, Old Testament narrative, the Prophets, Psalms, Wisdom, and Revelation. Fee and Stuart also suggest good commentaries on each biblical book. They write as conservative scholars who personally recognize Scripture as God's Word for their daily lives.

Jensen, Irving L. *Independent Bible Study* (Moody, 1963), and *Enjoy Your Bible* (Moody, 1962).

The former is a comprehensive introduction to the inductive Bible study method, especially the use of synthetic charts. The latter is a simpler introduction to the subject.

Wald, Oletta. *The Joy of Discovery in Bible Study* (Augsburg, 1975).

Wald focuses on issues such as how to observe all that is in a text, how to ask questions of a text, how to use grammar and passage structure to see the writer's point, and so on. Very helpful on these subjects.

Other titles in the *Lifechange* series you may be interested in: